Rati␣
Behav␣

D0084405

Rational Emotive Behaviour Therapy (REBT) encourages the client to focus on their emotional problems in order to understand, challenge and change the irrational beliefs that underpin these problems. REBT can help clients to strengthen conviction in their alternative rational beliefs by acting in ways that are consistent with them and thus encourage a healthier outlook.

This accessible and direct guide introduces the reader to REBT while indicating how it is different from other approaches within the broad cognitive behavioural therapy spectrum. Divided into two sections; *The Distinctive Theoretical Features of REBT* and *The Distinctive Practical Features of REBT*, this book presents concise, straightforward information in 30 key points derived from the author's own experience in the field.

Rational Emotive Behaviour Therapy: Distinctive Features will be invaluable to both experienced clinicians, and those new to the field. It will appeal to psychotherapists and counsellors, together with students and practitioners who are keen to learn how REBT can be differentiated from the other approaches to CBT.

Windy Dryden is Professor of Psychotherapeutic Studies at Goldsmiths College, London.

Cognitive-behavioural therapy (CBT) occupies a central position in the move towards evidence-based practice and is frequently used in the clinical environment. Yet there is no one universal approach to CBT and clinicians speak of first-, second-, and even third-wave approaches.

This series provides straightforward, accessible guides to a number of CBT methods, clarifying the distinctive features of each approach. The series editor, Windy Dryden, successfully brings together experts from each discipline to summarise the 30 main aspects of their approach divided into theoretical and practical features.

The CBT Distinctive Features Series will be essential reading for psychotherapists, counsellors, and psychologists of all orientations who want to learn more about the range of new and developing cognitive-behavioural approaches.

Titles in the series:

For further information about this series please visit
www.routledgementalhealth.com/cbt-distinctive-features

Rational Emotive Behaviour Therapy

Distinctive Features

Windy Dryden

Routledge
Taylor & Francis Group

LONDON AND NEW YORK

First published 2009 by Routledge
27 Church Road, Hove, East Sussex BN3 2FA

Simultaneously published in the USA and Canada
by Routledge
270 Madison Avenue, New York, NY 10016

Routledge is an imprint of the Taylor & Francis Group,
an informa business

Typeset in Times by Garfield Morgan,
Swansea, West Glamorgan
Printed and bound in Great Britain by
TJ International Ltd, Padstow, Cornwall
Cover design by Sandra Heath

This publication has been produced with paper manufactured to
strict environmental standards and with pulp derived from
sustainable forests.

British Library Cataloguing in Publication Data
A catalogue record for this book is available from the British Library

Library of Congress Cataloging in Publication Data
Dryden, Windy.
   Rational emotive behaviour therapy : distinctive features /
Windy Dryden.
       p. ; cm.
   Includes bibliographical references and index.
   ISBN 978-0-415-43085-2 (hardback) – ISBN 978-0-415-43086-9
(pbk.) 1. Rational emotive behavior therapy. I. Title.
   [DNLM: 1. Psychotherapy, Rational-Emotive–methods. 2. Behavior
Therapy–methods. 3. Emotions. WM 420.5.P8 D799rb 2009]
   RC489.R3D7888 2009
   616.89'14–dc22

                                                        2008016707

ISBN: 978-0-415-43085-2 (hbk)
ISBN: 978-0-415-43086-9 (pbk)

This book is dedicated to the life and legacy of Dr Albert Ellis, the founder of REBT

Contents

Introduction

At the time of writing (February, 2008), the cognitive-behaviour therapies are in the ascendancy in the psychotherapeutic spectrum. CBT approaches are the most commonly cited among evidence-based treatments and in Britain the National Institute for Clinical Excellence (NICE) recommends CBT more often than other therapeutic approaches in the treatment of a variety of psychological disorders. And yet, within the broad CBT spectrum, there exists a number of approaches that include the so-called first wave, second wave and now third wave CBT-based therapies. Thus, to say that all CBT therapies are equivalent places too much emphasis on their similarities and too little on their differences.

Over a quarter of a century ago, Ellis (1980a) addressed the issue of the place of REBT in the larger CBT spectrum by distinguishing between two types of REBT. The first, variously known as specialised or "elegant" REBT focused on the features that Ellis and other leading (past and present) REBT writers (e.g. Dryden, 2002; Grieger & Boyd, 1980; Wessler & Wessler, 1980) regard as preferential in the treatment of a variety of psychological disorders. The second, variously known as general and the more pejorative "inelegant" REBT was regarded by Ellis as synonymous with the broader field of CBT so that anything that falls under the rubric of CBT can be regarded as (general) REBT.

REBT therapists have privately recognised that specialised REBT, which will be discussed in this book, has its limits, although a full examination of these limits and the conditions under which its effectiveness is questioned has not been fully discussed in the clinical REBT literature let alone been the subject of empirical enquiry.

The fact that REBT can straddle two areas, its specific area and the wider CBT area, can be seen as having great pragmatic value. Thus, when it suits, REBT therapists can emphasise specific REBT and when it suits they can also claim that general REBT is really identical with CBT, thus allowing REBT therapists to align themselves with the great advantages of practising an evidence-based CBT approach.

The issue of there being two REBTs recently surfaced in the aftermath of events at the Albert Ellis Institute, which led to the founder's disengagement from the Institute that bears his name. Among the very many issues that this very sad situation raised were concerns about what constitutes REBT and the position of the Albert Ellis Institute with respect to how it described its training and clinical services. In this respect complaints were made that AEI had "watered down" REBT in the institute's training and clinical programmes. Observers on the relevant discussion boards have noted that the institute's website at various times mentioned REBT and CBT together, sometimes reversing this order.

These events and contexts called for a re-evaluation of the distinctive nature of REBT, which I have carried out here. Please note that in the present work, I will concern myself with the distinctive features of specific REBT. Thus when I use the term "REBT" in this book I refer to specific REBT (unless stated otherwise). In doing so, it is hoped that this will stimulate research to be carried out on the major theoretical and clinical hypotheses derived from (specific) REBT as well as on its therapeutic effectiveness.

Windy Dryden
London & Eastbourne
February, 2008

Part 1

THE DISTINCTIVE THEORETICAL FEATURES OF REBT

1

Post-modern relativism

Rational emotive behaviour therapy (REBT) is largely and distinctively based on the major principles of post-modernism and relativism. Enshrined in these principles is the major idea that there is no absolute truth and that so-called "reality" has to be viewed and understood within the context in which it occurs. However, this does not mean that all constructions are deemed to be equal; indeed, far from it. What it does mean is that people need to be sceptical of accounts of phenomena since the account may say as much or in some cases more about the account giver than about the account given.

This is an important point for therapists. Clients will often give an account of an experience and may invite therapists to validate the accuracy of their way of viewing the relevant event as well as how they felt about the event. REBT therapists do not initially get involved in discussions of the accuracy or otherwise of clients' perceptions and interpretations, preferring to encourage clients to assume temporarily that their interpretations are correct so to identify their beliefs about the said event. The beliefs are deemed to be more influential in determining their emotional responses to the events than their interpretations. What REBT therapists are in effect saying here is that there may be different ways of viewing what happened to you and it may not be possible or even relevant to discover the truth of what happened to you. So, let's not get caught up in the pursuit of absolute truth and instead assume, at least temporarily, that you were correct in your views so we can help you to identify and deal with the beliefs about what you think happened to you since these beliefs (as we will see) are of prime importance in explaining your response to this event.

When REBT therapists do address the issues of the truth or otherwise of their clients' interpretations of "reality" (and we tend to do this after we have helped them to identify and deal with the rigid and extreme beliefs that lie, according to REBT, at the core of their responses), we encourage them to test their interpretations against the available data (as do therapists from Beck's cognitive therapy). In doing so, we further encourage them to accept as "true" the interpretation that has most supporting data. This is known as the probabilistic approach because we are encouraging clients to accept the interpretation or hunch that is "true" on probabilistic grounds. If this interpretation was a horse in a race, it would be the favourite. However, and this is why this analogy that I have chosen is a good one, REBT therapists recognise that favourites do not always win races and that sometimes rank outsiders can win. Thus, while we encourage clients to accept as "probably true" the interpretation of an experience that has the most supportive evidence, we recognise and teach our clients to recognise that we and they may well be wrong and that a more fanciful hunch may better explain what happened. Yet, often it is not possible to tell. For these reasons, REBT therapists are not as interested in what happened to their clients as they are in their clients' beliefs about what they think happened to them.

REBT also holds a relativistic position about itself and its own propositions. Thus, it holds that its positions may have validity, but not in any absolutistic sense and that these ideas do have to be viewed within context. Its ideas may prove false in the years to come. It is interesting to note, therefore, that in the same way that REBT therapists encourage their clients to take themselves and their lives seriously, but not too seriously, they adopt the same attitude to REBT itself!

The philosophy enshrined in post-modern relativism is nicely encapsulated in the following quote by Jacques Barzun:

> Let us face a pluralistic world in which there are no universal churches, no single remedy for all diseases, no one way to

teach or write or sing, no magic diet, no world poets, and no chosen races, but only the wretched and wonderfully diversified human race.

(1964, p. 184)

2

REBT's position on human nature and other theoretical emphases: Distinctiveness in the mix

As Hjelle and Ziegler (1992) have argued, all personality theories are based on assumptions about human nature. REBT is based on a theory of personality which Ellis (1978) first outlined at the end of the 1970s. In this Point I will outline REBT's position on the basic assumptions about human nature underpinning its personality theory. I will also consider REBT's position on a range of philosophical and theoretical ideas other than that of post-modern relativism, which I discussed in Point 1. REBT's distinctiveness is not to be seen in any *one* of its following positions. Rather, its distinctiveness resides in their *mix*.

REBT's basic assumptions about human nature: Ziegler's approach

Ziegler (2000) has outlined the basic assumptions concerning human nature that underlie REBT's personality theory. This appears in Figure 1. I include Ziegler's views here since he is both an REBT practitioner and a leading personality theorist who co-wrote a standard text on personality theories (Hjelle & Ziegler, 1992). It is not known the extent to which his is a consensus view among REBT therapists, but Ziegler's views, given his status as an internationally respected personality theorist, carry the weight of authority.

Hjelle and Ziegler's (1992) nine basic assumptions concerning human nature that underpin all personality theories are:

Freedom – Determinism

How much internal freedom do people have and how much are they determined by external and internal (e.g. biological) factors?

Rationality – Irrationality

To what extent are people primarily rational, directing themselves through reason, or to what extent are they guided by irrational factors?

Holism – Elementalism

To what extent are people best comprehended as a whole or to what extent by being broken down into their constituent parts?

Constitutionalism – Environmentalism

To what extent are people the result of constitutional factors and to what extent are they products of environmental influences?

Changeability – Unchangeablity

To what extent are people capable of fundamental change over time?

Subjectivity – Objectivity

To what extent are people influenced by subjective factors and to what extent by external, objective factors?

Proactivity – Reactivity

To what extent do people generate their behaviour internally (proactivity) and to what extent do they respond to external stimuli (reactivity)?

Homeostasis – Heterostasis

To what extent are humans motivated primarily to reduce tensions and maintain an inner homeostasis and to what extent are they motivated to actualise themselves?

Knowability – Unknowability

To what extent is human nature fully knowable?

	Strong	Moderate	Slight	Mid-range	Slight	Moderate	Strong	
Freedom		■						Determinism
Rationality				■				Irrationality
Holism		■						Elementalism
Constitutionalism	■							Environmentalism
Changeability		■						Unchangeability
Subjectivity	■							Objectivity
Proactivity	■							Reactivity
Homeostasis				■				Heterostasis
Knowability						■		Unknowability

Figure 1 REBT's position on the nine basic assumptions concerning human nature (the shaded areas indicate the degree to which REBT favours one of the two human bipolar extremes). Reprinted with permission from Ziegler (2000)

Phenomenological and stoic emphases

REBT agrees, in large part, with the phenomenologists that we respond to events not as they are but more by how we see them. It also agrees, in large part, with the Stoic philosopher, Epictetus, who said that, "Men are disturbed not by things but by their views of things". These two emphases show how much REBT stresses cognition in human disturbance and health. However, as I make clear in Point 4, REBT emphasises in particular the role of rigid and extreme beliefs in human disturbance, which the phenomenologists and the Stoics do not. Thus, we have updated Epictetus's dictum to read:

People are disturbed not by things, but by the rigid and extreme beliefs that they hold about things.

Although REBT has changed its name twice since its establishment as Rational Therapy in 1955 (it became Rational-Emotive Therapy in 1962 and Rational Emotive Behaviour Therapy in 1993), it has always maintained the cognitive (Rational) dimension in its name.

Affective–experiential emphasis

While it agrees with Epictetus in the above respect, REBT does not go along with another Stoic view that we should strive to develop non-emotional responses to life adversities. In this regard, REBT is highly affective in emphasis and encourages people to have passionate positive *and* negative responses to things that are important to them, as long as these responses are healthy. This even includes strong negative responses to significant life adversities like loss. For example, to feel very sad when one loses a loved one is healthy. I will discuss REBT's distinctive view on the differences between healthy and unhealthy negative emotions later (Point 8). Rational Therapy was renamed Rational-Emotive Therapy because many people, believed, erroneously, that the therapy neglected emotion. This was not the case then and it is not the case now.

REBT also has an experiential element in that it advocates that people do fully experience their feelings. However, REBT holds that fully experiencing unhealthy negative feelings is not curative in itself, but is useful in that it helps the person to identify the irrational beliefs that underpin these feelings.

Behavioural emphasis

When Rational-Emotive Therapy (RET) became Rational Emotive Behaviour Therapy (REBT) in 1993, it was again because Ellis considered that people thought, again erroneously, that RET neglected behaviour. This was again incorrect. REBT argues that people are at their happiest when they are actively pursuing their personally meaningful goals and when they disturb themselves they often act in ways that deepen this disturbance.

Psychological interactionism

So far, I have outlined REBT's cognitive, emotional and behavioural emphases. It also adheres strongly to the principle of psychological interactionism, which argues that cognition, emotion and behaviour are not separate psychological systems, rather, they are overlapping processes and that when we think in terms of cognition, for example, we should also think of the affective (emotional) and behavioural (actual behaviours or action tendencies) components of these cognitions (Ellis, 1994). Indeed, REBT theory has emphasised this principle of psychological interactionism from its very inception (Ellis, 1962). Ellis has always urged REBT therapists to target all three systems in the change process and in particular has always advocated that without corresponding behavioural change, affective and cognitive change is transitory (Ellis, 1962). The misconception that REBT neglects behavioural change prompted Ellis to rebrand Rational-Emotive Therapy (RET) as Rational Emotive Behaviour Therapy (REBT) in 1993.

Psychodynamic features

Although REBT was created, in part, out of Ellis's disaffection with psychoanalysis, it is easy to assume that as a result REBT has dispensed with all psychodynamic insights. This is not the case. Thus, REBT therapists do agree with our psychodynamic colleagues that humans are influenced by unconscious ideas. However, we hold that, in the main, these ideas can be relatively easily discovered and brought to the client's conscious mind and are not deeply buried within the client's psyche requiring a long period of exploration to be made conscious.

Also, we agree with our psychodynamic colleagues that humans erect defences to protect themselves from threats to their ego (Freud, 1937). Actually, we go beyond this idea and argue that humans also erect defensive manoeuvres to protect themselves from threats to non-ego aspects of their personal domain.

Constructivistic emphasis

Ellis (1994) has argued that REBT is best seen as one of the constructivistic cognitive therapies. In REBT, the constructivistic focus is seen in the emphasis that REBT places on the active role that humans play in constructing their irrational beliefs and the distorted inferences that they frequently bring to emotional episodes. I will discuss this in more detail in Point 14.

Existential–humanistic emphasis

REBT has an existential–humanistic outlook, which is intrinsic to it and which is omitted by most other approaches to CBT. Thus, it sees people "as holistic, goal-directed individuals who have importance in the world just because they are human and alive; it unconditionally accepts them with their limitations; and it particularly focuses upon their experiences and values, including their self-actualising potentialities" (Ellis, 1980a, p. 327). It also shares the views of ethical humanism by encouraging people to emphasise human interest (self and social) over the interests of deities, material objects and lower animals.

General semantics emphasis

General semantics theory (GST) holds that people are influenced by the language that they employ to others and to themselves and that when we use imprecise language we are influenced for the worse (Korzybski, 1933). Thus, general semantics theory and REBT share a common goal in identifying such imprecise language forms as over-generalisations, always–never thinking and the "is" of predication and of identity and helping people to change them.

As noted earlier in this Point, because of its interactional or multifaceted view of mental events REBT does not neglect emotion and behaviour. However, as S. Nielsen (2006, personal communication) has observed:

> Examination of language offers the advantages of representing rigid irrational beliefs in the symbolic form of language where the belief is more easily examined and manipulated. While "should" is not always an indicator of a rigid belief (e.g. "It should rain by April 30th"), if it is used as a synonym for "must" it is an indicator for a rigid belief. The words and phrases "should", "ought", "must", "have to", "got to", "need to", and "supposed to"; "awful", "horrible", "unbearable", "terrible"; and "better person", "bad person", "jerk", "saint"; all can become useful foci for intervention, depending on the client's particular beliefs.

This means that such language is only indicative of the presence of irrational beliefs and that it is not inevitable that when clients use such seemingly irrational language they are necessarily thinking irrationally. As general semanticists note, the map is not the territory and thus the meaning underpinning words is of more interest to REBT therapists than the words themselves. Having said that, there may be some therapeutic benefit in encouraging clients to change their language in a comprehensive approach to helping them to think rationally.

REBT differs from GST in that it helps people to see that their imprecise language (e.g. "He is a jerk") frequently stems from their rigid beliefs and that it is easier to think in more precise ways when one has first changed one's rigid beliefs to flexible beliefs (see Point 21). In addition, REBT places more emphasis on the role of behaviour in helping people to think more precisely than does GST.

Systemic emphasis

REBT agrees with systems approaches to psychotherapy that people need to be understood within context. Thus, REBT holds that people are both influenced by and influence the interpersonal systems in which they live. However, REBT also states that ultimately such systems and the interpersonal inter-actions that occur within them only contribute to our clients' disturbances they do not determine them. The basic REBT point is as outlined in Point 3: "People are disturbed not by the systems in which they live, but by the rigid and extreme views that they take of these systems".

REBT is against religiosity not religion

Albert Ellis regarded himself as a probabilistic atheist, but held that religious belief is not an obstacle to the effective practice of REBT. The only time religious belief is an obstacle in REBT is when the REBT therapist brings his or her devout religious beliefs to the therapy. However, what is damaging here is the devoutness of the belief, not the religious content and the intrusion of any devout therapist belief in the therapeutic process is counter-therapeutic even when the content of the devout belief is REBT theory! Thus it is not religion that is the problem here; it is religiosity (Ellis, 1983a).

REBT theory does have echoes in certain religious thought. For example the principle of other-acceptance in REBT (see Points 7 and 10) is similar to the Christian doctrine of accepting the sinner, but not the sin, although the idea that a person can be *a* sinner is problematic in REBT since this involves labelling a person with his behaviour.

3

REBT's distinctive ABC model

Many approaches to CBT make use of what is known as the ABC model. In its general form "A" stands for an event, "B" stands for the belief about this event and "C" stands for the consequences (most usually emotional) of holding the belief at "B".

However, when we consider specific REBT, we see that a different, more sophisticated ABC model emerges. I have called this model the Situational ABC model. In this model, the ABC factors occur within a situational context. Within this context "A" stands for the aspect of the situation to which we respond (at "C"), "C" stands for this response and "B" stands for the beliefs we hold about the "A" that largely accounts for our response at "C".

If we consider this model more closely we find the following:

1 "A" is usually inferential in nature. An inference is a hunch or interpretation about reality, which goes beyond the data at hand and may be accurate or inaccurate. Aaron T. Beck (e.g. 1976), the founder of cognitive therapy has written about the most common inferences that are associated with different emotions and REBT therapists (e.g. Dryden, 2002) have drawn on his work in outlining the kinds of inferences at "A" associated with common emotional disorders at "C" (e.g. threat in anxiety, loss in depression, transgression of a valued personal rule in anger).
2 As we will soon see, beliefs at "B" are either irrational (rigid and extreme) or rational (flexible and non-extreme).
3 "C" stands for the consequences of the beliefs held at "B". There are three such consequences: emotional, behavioural (overt actions or action tendencies) and thinking.

It is worth knowing in this context that when we consider some of the complexity of REBT's ABC framework, we discover that cognitions appear throughout the model. Thus, inferential cognitions occur at "A" and at "C" and beliefs occur at "B". This is exemplified below:

A = "I am beginning to lose control of my breathing" (inference at "A").

B = "I must gain control of my breathing right now and it would be awful if I don't" (irrational belief at "B").

C = "If I don't I will have a heart attack and die!" (inference at "C").

Having outlined REBT's distinctive ABC model, I will now discuss in the following two Points what is perhaps REBT's most distinctive contribution; its position on irrational and rational beliefs at "B".

4

Rigidity is at the core of psychological disturbance

All approaches to psychological treatment are based on how psychological disturbance is conceptualised. A major distinctive theoretical feature of REBT is that people are disturbed not by things but by the rigid views that they take of them. This updated version of Epictetus's famous dictum ("Men are disturbed not by things but by the views that they take of them") specifies the type of cognitions that REBT considers to lie at the core of disturbance, namely rigid beliefs. Rigidity (also referred to as religiosity, dogmatism, absolutism and demandingness in the REBT literature) takes the form of musts, demands, absolute shoulds, needs, have to's, got to's, among others. These musts have three foci: self, others and life, as in:

- "I must . . . ."
- "You (others) must . . . ."
- "Life must . . . ."

Rigid beliefs, for the most part, tend to be based on our desires. Indeed, REBT stresses that it is a basic design feature of human beings that we have desires. We are either oriented towards something or away from it. Thus, we don't operate purely on the inferences that we make about the world; rather we hold beliefs (i.e. hold a positive stance or negative stance) concerning what we infer. According to the theory of REBT it is these beliefs that have a greater impact on how we feel and act than the inferences that we make.

Our preferences vary in strength from mild to very strong. REBT theory holds that the stronger our preferences, the more likely we are to transform these preferences into rigidities. Thus, if I mildly want to beat you at tennis, I am unlikely to transform this into a rigid belief. However, if my desire to beat you at tennis is very strong then I am more likely to (but, of course, not guaranteed to) transform this strong desire into a rigid belief ("I really want to beat you at tennis therefore I have to do so"). In this respect REBT theory makes clear that rigidity is a quality separate from strength of desire. Multiplication of "really" in the above sentence will not become a demand: Thus, "I really, really, really, really, very, very much want to beat you at tennis" will never on its own become a demand, "I must beat you at tennis". It takes the person to arbitrarily change their non-dogmatic desire to a rigid demand to achieve this transformation.

The holding of rigid beliefs represents our attempt to make certain events magically happen. If, indeed, our rigid beliefs had these effects, then it might be sensible for us to hold them. So, if by holding the rigid belief: "I must pass my driving test", I was guaranteed to pass it, then it would be sensible for me to hold this belief. Sadly, of course, the very holding of a rigid belief does not influence reality. It only influences our responses to reality.

Conversely, the holding of rigid beliefs is our attempt to exclude the possibility of certain events from happening, even though we are not convinced that they can be so excluded. Thus, when I believe: "I must pass my driving test", I am attempting to exclude the possibility of failure. As such rigid beliefs are inconsistent with reality in that there is almost always the possibility that such events will occur and, at some level, I know this, I feel disturbed about the prospect of failure. If by believing that I must pass my driving test, I was convinced that I had excluded the possibility of failing it then I would not be disturbed about failure because I would be sure that it could not happen. The fact that I am anxious about failure when I hold a rigid belief about it means that I am not convinced that my rigid belief will do what it is designed to do.

5

Flexibility is at the core of psychological health

All approaches to psychological treatment also specify, either explicitly or implicitly, the factors that explain psychological health. If rigidity is deemed to be at the core of psychological disturbance in REBT, it follows that flexibility is deemed to be at the core of psychological health. The appropriate dictum might be: "People react healthily to events when they hold flexible views of (or more accurately, beliefs about) these events". This dictum specifies the type of cognitions that are at the core of psychological health, namely flexible beliefs. Flexibility builds upon the basic human fact that we form preferences about things and takes the form of *non-dogmatic* preferences, desires, wishes, wants, among others. Flexible beliefs have two components. In the first component (which I call the "asserted preference" component), we assert our preferences about what we want to happen or not happen. In the second component (which I call the "negated demand" component) we acknowledge that we do not have to get what we want. As with musts, these non-dogmatic preferences have three foci: self, others and life, as in:

- "I want X to happen (or not happen) . . . but, I don't have to get my desire met . . . ."
- "I would prefer it if you (others) . . . but you (they) don't have to do what I prefer . . . ."
- "It would be desirable if life . . . but it doesn't have to be that way . . . ."

When we hold a flexible belief, we are making clear to ourselves and, if appropriate, to others what we desire. However, when we hold a flexible belief (rather than a rigid belief) we are not attempting to make certain events magically happen. Rather, we are being realistic since both components that comprise a flexible belief are consistent with reality. We can generally prove that we hold a desire and can also prove that we don't have to get our desire met. Thus when I hold the flexible belief: "I want to pass my driving test, but I don't have to do so", I can prove that I want to pass my driving test, by giving reasons why it would be good for me to do so (e.g. "I would be less reliant on public transport", "I could go for long drives over the weekend", etc.) but I am also acknowledging that this belief does not guarantee that I must pass it.

Also, unlike with rigid beliefs, when we hold flexible beliefs, we do not attempt to exclude the possibility of certain events from happening. Indeed, we overtly acknowledge this possibility. Thus, when I believe: "I want to pass my driving test, but I don't have to do so", I am not attempting to exclude the possibility of failure. Rather, I am acknowledging the possibility that I may fail. As such, flexible beliefs are consistent with reality in that there is almost always the possibility that undesirable events will happen.

6

Extreme beliefs are derived from rigid beliefs

Another distinctive theoretical feature of REBT is that there are deemed to be three extreme beliefs that are derived from rigid beliefs. These are known as awfulising beliefs, low frustration tolerance (LFT) beliefs and depreciation beliefs. I will consider these one by one.

Awfulising beliefs

Awfulising beliefs are extreme ideas that we hold about how bad it is when our rigid demands are not met. Thus, as stated above, awfulising beliefs are derivatives from our rigid beliefs when these aren't met. In the following examples the demands are listed in parentheses:

- "(I must be approved) . . . It is terrible if I am not approved."
- "(You must treat me fairly) . . . It is awful when you treat me unfairly."
- "(Life must be comfortable) . . . It is the end of the world when life is uncomfortable."

Awfulising beliefs stem from the demand that things must not be as bad as they are and are extreme in the sense that we believe *at the time* something very much like following:

1 nothing could be worse;
2 the event in question is worse than 100% bad; and
3 no good could possibly come from this bad event.

21

Low frustration tolerance (LFT) beliefs

Low frustration tolerance (LFT) beliefs are extreme ideas that we hold about the tolerability of events when our demands are not met. Thus LFT beliefs are derivatives from our rigid beliefs when these aren't met. In the following examples the demands are listed in parentheses.

- "(I must be approved) . . . I can't bear it if I am not approved."
- "(You must treat me fairly) . . . It is intolerable when you don't treat me fairly."
- "(Life must be comfortable) . . . I can't stand it when it is uncomfortable."

LFT beliefs stem from the demand that things must not be as frustrating or uncomfortable as they are and are extreme in the sense that we believe *at the time* something very much like following:

1 If the frustration or discomfort continues to exist it is too hard for me to do anything about it.
2 I will die or disintegrate if the frustration or discomfort continues to exist.
3 I will lose the capacity to experience happiness if the frustration or discomfort continues to exist.

Depreciation beliefs

Depreciation beliefs are extreme ideas that we hold about self, other(s) and/or life when our rigid beliefs are not met. As such, and as stated above, depreciation beliefs are derivatives from our unmet rigid demands. In the following examples the demands are listed in parentheses.

- "(I must be approved) . . . I am worthless if I am not approved."

- "(You must treat me fairly) . . . You are a bad person if you don't treat me fairly."
- "(Life must be comfortable) . . . Life is bad if it is uncomfortable."

Depreciation beliefs stem from the demand that we, others or life must be as we want them to be and are extreme in the sense that we believe *at the time* something very much like following:

1   A person (self or other) can legitimately be given a single global rating that defines their essence and the worth of a person is dependent upon conditions that change (e.g. our worth goes up when we do well and goes down when we don't do well).
2   Life can legitimately be given a single rating that defines its essential nature and that the value of life varies according to what happens within it (e.g. the value of life goes up when something fair occurs and goes down when something unfair happens).
3   A person can be rated on the basis of one of his or her aspects and life can be rated on the basis of one of its aspects.

7

Non-extreme beliefs are derived from flexible beliefs

In the same way as REBT theory states that three extreme beliefs are derived from rigid beliefs, it holds that three non-extreme beliefs are derived from flexible beliefs. These are known as anti-awfulising beliefs, high frustration tolerance (HFT) beliefs and acceptance beliefs. I will now consider these one by one.

Anti-awfulising beliefs

Anti-awfulising beliefs are non-extreme ideas we hold about how bad it is when our non-dogmatic preferences are not met. Thus, non-awfulising beliefs are derivatives from our flexible beliefs when these non-dogmatic preferences aren't met. In the following examples the non-dogmatic preferences are in parentheses.

- "(I want to be approved, but I don't have to be) . . . It's bad if I am not approved, but not terrible."
- "(I want you to treat me fairly, but regrettably you don't have to do so) . . . When you don't treat me fairly it's really bad, but not awful."
- "(I very much want life to be comfortable, but unfortunately it doesn't have to be that way) . . . If life is uncomfortable, that's very bad, but not the end of the world."

Two components of anti-awfulising beliefs

If you look carefully at the anti-awfulising beliefs (i.e. the ones that are not in parentheses) you will see that they are made up of two components.

"Asserted badness" component

The first component puts forward the idea that it is bad when we don't get what we want and this is what I call the "asserted badness" component.

- "It's bad if I am not approved . . . ."
- "When you don't treat me fairly, it's really bad . . . ."
- "If life is uncomfortable, that's very bad . . . ."

"Negated awfulising" component

The second component acknowledges that while it is bad when we don't get what we want, it is not terrible, awful or the end of the world. This is what I call the "negated awfulising" component. These are shown in italics below:

- "It's bad if I am not approved, *but not terrible.*"
- "When you don't treat me fairly it's really bad, *but not awful.*"
- "If life is uncomfortable, that's very bad, *but not the end of the world.*

Anti-awfulising beliefs stem from the non-dogmatic preference that we would like things not to be as bad as they are, but that doesn't mean that they must not be as bad. These beliefs are non-extreme in the sense that we believe *at the time* something very much like the following:

1   Things could always be worse.
2   The event in question is less than 100% bad.
3   Good could come from this bad event.

High frustration tolerance (HFT) beliefs

High frustration tolerance (HFT) beliefs are non-extreme ideas that you hold about the tolerability of events when your non-dogmatic preferences are not met. Thus, HFT beliefs are derivatives from your non-dogmatic preferences when these are not met. In the following examples the non-dogmatic preferences are in parentheses.

- "(I want to be approved, but I don't have to be) . . . When I am not approved it is difficult to bear, but I can bear it and it's worth bearing because I don't want to live my life worried about disapproval."
- "(I want you to treat me fairly, but regrettably you don't have to do so) . . . When you don't treat me fairly it's really hard to tolerate, but I can tolerate it and it's worth it to me to do so because I don't want to be overly affected about what you do."
- "(I very much want life to be comfortable, but unfortunately it doesn't have to be the way I want it to be) . . . If life is uncomfortable, that's hard to stand, but I can stand it and it is in my best interests to do so because I want to get on with life."

Three components of high frustration tolerance (HFT) beliefs

If you look carefully at the high frustration tolerance beliefs (i.e. the ones that are not in parentheses) you will see that they are made up of three components.

"Asserted struggle" component

The first component puts forward the idea that it is difficult tolerating not getting what we want and is what I call the "asserted struggle" component.

- "When I am not approved, it is difficult to bear . . . ."
- "When you don't treat me fairly, it's really hard to tolerate . . . ."
- "If life is uncomfortable, that's hard to stand . . . ."

"Negated unbearability" component

The second component acknowledges that while it is a struggle to put up with what we don't want, it is possible for us to do so and that it isn't unbearable. This is what I call the "negated unbearability" component. This component is shown in italics in the examples below:

- "When I am not approved it is difficult to bear, *but I can bear it . . . .*"
- "When you don't treat me fairly it's really hard to tolerate, *but I can tolerate it . . . .*"
- "If life is uncomfortable, that's hard to stand, *but I can stand it . . . .*"

"Worth bearing" component

The third component addresses the point that it is often worth it to you to tolerate the situation where you don't get what you want. This is what I call the "worth bearing" component. This component is shown in italics in the examples below. Note that in each case the reason why it is worth tolerating is specified.

- "When I am not approved it is difficult to bear, but I can bear it *and it's worth bearing because I don't want to live my life worried about disapproval.*"
- "When you don't treat me fairly it's really hard to tolerate, but I can tolerate it *and it's worth it to me to do so because I don't want to be overly affected about what you do.*"
- "If life is uncomfortable, that's hard to stand, but I can stand it *and it is in my best interests to do so because I want to get on with life.*"

HFT beliefs stem from the non-dogmatic preference that it is undesirable when things are as frustrating or uncomfortable as they are, but unfortunately things don't have to be different. It is non-extreme in the sense that we believe *at the time* something very much like the following:

1   It is hard, but not too hard if the frustration or discomfort continues to exist.
2   I will struggle if the frustration or discomfort continues to exist, but I will neither die nor disintegrate.
3   I will not lose the capacity to experience happiness if the frustration or discomfort continues to exist, although this capacity will be temporarily diminished.
4   The frustration or discomfort is worth tolerating.

Acceptance beliefs

Acceptance beliefs are non-extreme ideas that we hold about self, other(s) and/or the world when we don't get what we want, but do not demand that we have to get what we want. As such, acceptance beliefs are derivatives from our non-dogmatic preferences when these non-dogmatic preferences aren't met. In the following examples the non-dogmatic preferences are in parentheses:

•   "(I want to be approved, but I don't have to be) . . . When I am not approved that is bad, but I am not worthless. I am a fallible human being who is not being approved on this occasion."
•   "(I want you to treat me fairly, but regrettably you don't have to do so) . . . When you don't treat me fairly that is very unfortunate, but you are not a bad person. Rather, you are a fallible human being who is treating me unfairly."
•   "(I very much want life to be comfortable, but unfortunately it doesn't have to be the way I want it to be) . . . If life is uncomfortable it is only uncomfortable in this respect and doesn't prove that the world is a rotten place. The world is a complex place where many good, bad and neutral things happen."

29

Three components of acceptance beliefs

If you look carefully at the acceptance beliefs (i.e. the ones that are not in parentheses) you will see that they are made up of at least three components.

"Evaluation of a part of self, other or what has happened to self" component

The first component acknowledges that it is possible and realistic to evaluate a part of oneself, another person or what has happened to oneself as shown in italics below:

- When I am not approved *that is bad . . . .*
- When you don't treat me fairly *that is very regrettable . . . .*
- If life is uncomfortable *it is only uncomfortable in this respect . . . .*

"Negation of depreciation" component

The second component puts forward the idea that it is not possible to evaluate globally a person or life conditions when we don't get what we want. I call this the "negation of depreciation" component. These are shown in italics below:

- "When I am not approved that is bad, *but I am not worthless . . . ."*
- "When you don't treat me fairly that is very *regrettable, but you are not a bad person . . . ."*
- "If life is uncomfortable it is only uncomfortable in this respect *and doesn't prove that the world is a rotten place . . . ."*

"Assertion of acceptance" component

The third component asserts the idea that when we don't get what we want, this does not affect the fallibility of people and the complexity of life. This is what I call the "assertion of acceptance" component. These are shown in italics below:

- "When I am not approved that is bad, but I am not worthless. *I am a fallible human being who is not being approved on this occasion.*"
- "When you don't treat me fairly that is very regrettable, but you are not a bad person. *Rather you are a fallible human being who is treating me unfairly.*"
- "If life is uncomfortable it is only uncomfortable in this respect and doesn't prove that the world is a rotten place. *The world is a complex place where many good, bad and neutral things happen.*"

Acceptance beliefs are non-extreme in the sense that we believe *at the time* something very much like the following:

1 A person (self or other) cannot legitimately be given a single global rating that defines their essence and their worth, as far as they have it, and is not dependent upon conditions that change (e.g. my worth stays the same whether or not I do well).
2 The world cannot legitimately be given a single rating that defines its essential nature and that the value of the world does not vary according to what happens within it (e.g. the value of the world stays the same whether fairness exists at any given time or not).
3 It makes sense to rate discrete aspects of a person and of the world, but it does not make sense to rate a person or the world on the basis of these discrete aspects.

8

Distinction between unhealthy negative emotions (UNEs) and healthy negative emotions (HNEs)

REBT is unique among the cognitive-behavioural therapies in distinguishing between emotions that are negative in tone, but largely healthy in effect and emotions that are negative in tone and largely unhealthy in effect. The former are known as healthy negative emotions (HNEs) while the latter are known as unhealthy negative emotions (UNEs). Unfortunately, we do not have good words in the English language for UNEs and HNEs and thus, different REBT theorists have used different lexicons in this respect. My own (e.g. Dryden, 2002) is as follows:

UNEs	HNEs
Anxiety	Concern
Depression	Sadness
Guilt	Remorse
Shame	Disappointment
Hurt	Sorrow
Unhealthy anger	Healthy anger
Unhealthy jealousy	Healthy jealousy
Unhealthy envy	Healthy envy

REBT's distinction between UNEs and HNEs follows logically from REBT's position on the difference between irrational (i.e. rigid and extreme) beliefs and rational (i.e. flexible and non-extreme) beliefs. On the latter difference, REBT theory holds that rational and irrational beliefs are qualitatively different. This means that while a person holds a rational belief about an adversity, it is not possible for that person to hold an irrational belief about that adversity and vice versa. Now, according to

REBT theory, it is possible for a person to hold a rational belief about a negative activating event and the very next minute hold an irrational belief about that same event, but the contemporaneous holding of a rational belief with its irrational belief counterpart is not possible.

Now, in REBT, UNEs are deemed to stem from irrational beliefs about adversities while HNEs are deemed to stem from rational beliefs about these adversities. Since rational beliefs and irrational beliefs are held to be qualitatively different, it follows that UNEs are qualitatively different from HNEs. For example, using the above list, it is not possible for a person to feel anxious and concerned at the same time. This is why in REBT our goal is to help a person who feels anxious about an adversity to feel concerned about that adversity. Other approaches to CBT would consider it to be appropriate and legitimate to help a person feel less anxious about an adversity. REBT therapists would be reluctant to do this because the achievement of this goal would involve helping the person to hold their irrational belief with less intensity rather than think rationally.

As I mentioned earlier, we don't have a universally accepted lexicon that keenly discriminates UNEs from HNEs. Given this, REBT therapists do not rely on these words alone to help their clients to discriminate UNEs from HNEs. We also make use of the behavioural and thinking consequences of rational and irrational beliefs as well as the beliefs themselves. For example, let's suppose that a client is not sure whether he (in this case) was experiencing anxiety or concern in a given situation. You may help him to identify his emotion at C by identifying his belief (irrational in anxiety, rational in concern), the behaviour accompanying his emotion (avoiding the threat, for example, in anxiety, confronting the threat in concern) and/or his subsequent thinking (overestimating the negativity of the consequences if the threat were to materialise in anxiety; making a realistic estimation of these consequences in concern).

While less frequently mentioned in the literature, REBT theory also distinguishes between unhealthy positive emotions

(UPEs) and healthy positive emotions (HPEs). Unhealthy positive emotions (such as mania) tend to stem from rigid beliefs that are met and from the extreme beliefs that accompany these met rigid beliefs. For example if I believe that I must get promotion and I do in fact get it, then I may well conclude that it is wonderful that I did so and feel manic as a result. Although these manic feelings are positive in tone, they are largely unhealthy in effect in that they tend to lead people to act in disinhibited ways.

By contrast, healthy positive emotions (such as delight) tend to stem from non-dogmatic beliefs that are met and from the non-extreme beliefs that accompany these met non-dogmatic beliefs. For example if I believe that I want, but don't have to get, promotion and I do in fact get it, then I may well conclude that it is great (but not wonderful) that I did so and feel delight as a result. These feelings of delight are positive in tone and they are largely healthy in effect in that they tend to lead people to celebrate appropriately, rather than act in disinhibited ways.

9

Explaining why clients' inferences are highly distorted

One of the difficulties novice therapists have in practising REBT is in making sense of their clients' distorted inferences. They know that they are supposed to encourage their clients to assume temporarily that their inferences are true, but sometimes when they do this and these inferences are highly distorted, they run into great difficulty clinically. For example, let's suppose that a client reports that she (in this case) was panicking the night before. Not unreasonably, the novice REBT therapist asks the client what she was panicking about to which the client responds that she was most scared of dying from a heart attack. This, of course, is an inference, so the novice REBT knows not to challenge it, but to encourage the client to assume temporarily that she will die from a heart attack as a way of identifying and disputing her irrational beliefs about what the therapist thinks is an "A". And, indeed, from one perspective it is an "A", but it is also a thinking consequence of a prior irrational belief about a less distorted "A" and it is this standpoint that is more likely to yield the best results clinically in this given situation. This example shows that highly distorted inferences are often best conceptualised in REBT as cognitive consequences (i.e. "C") of rigid and extreme irrational beliefs about less distorted inferences at "A". While schema-focused therapy (e.g. Young & Klosko, 1993) also makes this point, only REBT does this in the context of the ABC framework for which it is known.

10

Position on human worth

REBT has a distinctive position on the issue of human worth. To be accurate it has two positions, one that it particularly espouses and another that is less favoured, but acceptable.

Its preferred position is that it makes little sense to say that as humans we have or lack worth. We exist in a social world and we have a choice to exist healthily or miserably, with or without due regard to our social groups and to our environment. We are happiest when we are actively pursuing goals that are meaningful. We do not need to consider ourselves worthwhile in order to be happy and since one of the sources of emotional disturbance is rooted in our tendency to view ourselves and others as conditionally worthwhile, conditional human worth interferes with our emotional wellbeing and happiness.

REBT considers that it is just as feasible to say that humans are worthless as it is to say that we are worthwhile. Assigning worth to humans is, therefore, a choice and if we decide to choose this position we are advised to choose a philosophy of unconditional worth rather than a philosophy of conditional worth as discussed below.

Conditional human worth

The philosophy of conditional human worth comprises a number of positions:

1   It implies that humans are simple organisms that merit a global evaluation.

2   It implies that a person's worth can go up and down based on the presence or absence of certain conditions deemed important to the person.
3   It makes the error of over-generalisation when it bases a person's worth on a single or small number of traits, characteristics and/or behaviours (e.g. "My acting poorly means that I am bad").
4   It implies that humans are perfectible.
5   It encourages emotional disturbance, which occurs when conditional, global evaluations of worth are assigned to humans.

Unconditional acceptance of humans

The preferred alternative to the philosophy of conditional human worth in REBT is the philosophy known as unconditional acceptance of humans. This philosophy comprises a number of positions:

1   It acknowledges that humans are a complex mixture of the good, the bad and the neutral and thus too complex to merit a global evaluation.
2   It states that a person can accept self or others unconditionally, i.e. whether or not certain desired conditions are present.
3   It avoids making the error of over-generalisation since the concept of complexity can incorporate positive, negative and neutral features (e.g. "My acting poorly does not mean that I am bad. I am complex as a human and can act poorly, well and neutrally").
4   It acknowledges the fallibility and non-perfectability of humans.
5   It protects people from emotional disturbance. Much (but far from all) emotional disturbance stems from assigning conditional, global evaluations of worth to humans. In

unconditional acceptance of humans, such assignations are not made.

Unconditional human worth

REBT theory advocates unconditional acceptance as the preferred healthy alternative to conditional human worth because it does not use the concept of worth with its attendant problems (mainly that it implies that humans can be globally rated as having worth). However, it has a fall-back less preferred alternative known as "unconditional human worth". This philosophy comprises a number of positions:

1   Humans can be given global evaluations with respect to worth.
2   It is best to give humans positive global evaluations with respect to worth.
3   These positive global evaluations remain in place no matter what and are therefore unconditional (e.g. "Even though I have acted poorly, I am worthwhile").
4   Humans are worthwhile as long as they are alive, fallible and human.

This position is vulnerable in the sense that it could just as easily be argued that humans are worthless for the above reasons. However, this position has pragmatic value and is especially useful with clients who do not understand or want to use the concept of unconditional acceptance of humans.

11

Distinction between ego and discomfort disturbance and health

Albert Ellis and other REBT theorists have proposed somewhat different approaches to distinguishing between different fundamental types of disturbance and health. In this Point I will review three such approaches which show REBT's distinctiveness.

Approach 1: Ego and discomfort disturbance and health

REBT is unique in the distinction that it makes between two fundamental forms of disturbance and health. I will consider the two fundamental disturbances first. These are ego disturbance and discomfort disturbance – or what I have called non-ego disturbance (Dryden, 1999).

Ellis first made this distinction clear in 1979–80, when he published an important two-part article on discomfort anxiety and contrasted this with ego anxiety (Ellis, 1979, 1980b).

Ego disturbance and discomfort disturbance

Ego disturbance
This disturbance takes the form of self-depreciation (see also above). This occurs when I make demands on myself and I fail to meet these demands. It involves: (a) the process of giving my "self" a global negative rating; and (b) "devil-ifying" myself as being bad or less worthy. This second process rests on a theological concept, and implies either that I am undeserving of pleasure on earth or that I should rot in hell as a subhuman (devil).

43

Ego disturbance is also found in demands on others (e.g. "You must treat me well or I am no good") and in demands on life conditions (e.g. "I must be promoted and if I am not I am useless").

Discomfort disturbance

This form of disturbance stems from the irrational belief, "I must feel comfortable and have comfortable life conditions". Conclusions that stem from this premise are (a) "It's awful when these life conditions do not exist" and (b) "I can't stand the discomfort when these life conditions do not exist". Discomfort disturbance occurs in different forms and is central to a full understanding of a number of emotional and behavioural disturbances such as unhealthy anger, agoraphobia, depression, procrastination and alcoholism. Discomfort disturbance usually gets in the way of people working persistently hard to effect productive psychological change and is thus a major form of "resistance" to change in psychotherapy.

It is useful to note that, according to REBT theory, demands made on other people either involve ego disturbance (for example "You must approve of me and if you don't it proves that I am less worthy") or discomfort disturbance (You must approve of me and give me what I must have and if you don't I can't bear it and you are no good for giving me such discomfort"), and thus do not represent a (third) fundamental human disturbance, since they include one or other of the two fundamental disturbances.

Ego health and discomfort tolerance

According to REBT theory there are two types of psychological health: ego health and discomfort tolerance.

Ego health

The most common form of ego health is unconditional self-acceptance (as discussed above). This occurs when I hold preferences about myself, but do not demand that I must achieve these preferences. When we accept ourselves, we acknowledge that we are fallible human beings who are constantly in flux and too complex to be given a single legitimate rating. REBT theory advocates that it is legitimate, and often helpful, to rate one's traits, behaviours, etc., but that it is not legitimate to rate one's self at all, even in a global positive manner, since positive self-rating tends to be conditional on doing good things, being loved and approved, and so on.

Ego health is also found in non-dogmatic preferences about others (e.g. "I want you to treat me well, but you do not have to do so. If you don't, I am the same fallible human being as I would be if you did treat me well") and in non-dogmatic preferences about life conditions (e.g. "I want to be promoted, but it isn't essential that I am. If I am not, I am not useless. I am acceptable as a human being with good, bad and neutral points").

Discomfort tolerance

This stems from the rational belief, "I want to feel comfortable and have comfortable life conditions, but I don't need to have such comfort in my life". Conclusions that stem from this premise are (a) "It's bad, but not awful when these life conditions do not exist" and (b) "I can stand the discomfort when these life conditions do not exist". Discomfort tolerance is central to dealing with a range of psychological problems and is a hallmark of what is known as psychological resilience (Reivich & Shatte, 2002) in that it encourages people to face up to life adversities and cope with them head on, with difficulty to be sure, particularly in the short term, but ultimately to good effect in the longer term. Discomfort tolerance also encourages people to work hard and to be persistent in effecting productive psychological change and its presence augurs well for change in psychotherapy. Finally, discomfort tolerance forms the basis of a philosophy of long-range hedonism: the pursuit of meaningful long-term goals while tolerating the deprivation of attractive short-term goals, which are self-defeating in the longer term.

According to REBT theory, non-dogmatic preferences about people either involve ego health (for example "I would like you to approve of me but you don't have to do so and if you don't I can still accept myself") or discomfort tolerance ("I want you to approve of me and give me what I must have, but you don't have to do so. If you don't, I can bear it"), and thus do not represent a distinct form of psychological health since they include one or other of the two fundamental types of psychological health.

Approach 2: Self-related, other-related and life-related disturbance and health

In his later writings, Ellis moved away from emphasising the distinction between ego and discomfort disturbance and health towards distinguishing between what I have called here self-related, other-related and life-related disturbance and health (e.g. Ellis, 2004). My view is that Ellis did this to capitalise on CBT's current interest in acceptance as a curative factor in bringing about therapeutic change.

USA, UOA and ULA

Drawing on his penchant for mnemonics, Ellis (2004) recently argued that a fundamental goal of REBT is to promote three types of acceptance: USA (unconditional self-acceptance), UOA (unconditional other-acceptance) and ULA (unconditional life-acceptance). I have already discussed these three forms of acceptance as non-extreme belief derivatives from flexible beliefs in Point 7.

SD, OD and LD

Extrapolating from Ellis's views on USA, UOA and ULA, we can say that REBT therapists now target three major problems for change:

- SD (self-depreciation) where the person is depreciating him- or herself in some way;
- OD (other-depreciation) where the person is depreciating another person or persons in some way; and
- LD (life-depreciation) where the person is depreciating life in some way.

Whether one conceptualises disturbance and health in terms of self vs. discomfort or in terms of its focus on self, other and life, it is my view that a distinctive and enduring feature of REBT is that both of these are deemed to stem from rigid beliefs and flexible beliefs respectively about:

1   ego and discomfort or
2   self, other(s) or life.

I have stressed this in Points 6 and 7.

Approach 3: Disturbance and health matrices

While the above two approaches cover similar ground they are not identical. Dryden, Gordon, and Neenan (1997) have made an attempt to integrate both these approaches by using 3×2 disturbance and health matrices.

The 3 × 2 disturbance matrix

Dryden et al. (1997) argued that it is possible to take the three basic "musts" (about self, others and life) and the two fundamental disturbances (i.e. ego and discomfort) to form a 3×2 disturbance matrix (see Figure 2). I will now discuss the six types of disturbance yielded by this matrix.

(A) Ego disturbance – Demands about self

In this type of disturbance, it is quite clear that the person concerned is making demands upon herself (in this case) and

47

	Ego	Discomfort
I must . . .	A	B
You must . . .	C	D
Life must . . .	E	F

Figure 2 The 3 × 2 disturbance matrix

the main issue is her attitude towards herself. The major derivative from the "must" is some aspect of self-depreciation, for example:

- "I must do well in my exams and if I don't, I'm no good."
- "I must be loved and approved by certain people in my life, and if I'm not, that proves I'm no good."

(B) Discomfort disturbance – Demands about self

Here, the person makes demands about herself, but the real issue concerns her attitude towards discomfort. For example:

- "If I don't obtain my degree, I might have to settle for some kind of tedious, manual job. I must achieve more than this and couldn't stand the hardship if I don't."

(C) Ego disturbance – Demands about others

In this example, the person is making demands about the behaviour (or its absence) of another, but the real issue centres round her attitude towards herself. This often occurs when the person is angry about the other person because that person's behaviour constitutes a threat to her self-esteem. For example:

- "If you don't treat me nicely, it proves that you don't think much of me. You must think well of me and if you don't, it means that I am no longer any good as a person."

(D) Discomfort disturbance – Demands about others

Here, the person is making demands upon others, but the real issue concerns the realm of discomfort. For example:

- "You must treat me nicely and look after me. I couldn't stand the hard life I'd be faced with if you do not."

(E) Ego disturbance – Demands about life conditions

On the surface, the person is making demands about some aspects of life conditions, but the real issue concerns her attitude towards herself. For example:

- "Life conditions under which I live must be easy for me. If they are not then that's just proof of my own worthlessness."

(F) Discomfort disturbance – Demands about life conditions

In this final kind of disturbance we are dealing with a more impersonal form of low frustration tolerance. This type of discomfort is frequently seen when people lose their temper with inanimate objects, or in situations requiring a fair amount of patience. For example:

- "I must not be frustrated by my car breaking down when I'm just about to use it. I am so frustrated, I cannot stand it."
- "When I join a queue for some service, I must be served quickly. I can't stand delays in getting what I want."

	Ego	Discomfort
I want . . . but I don't have to . . .	A	B
I want you to . . . but you don't have to . . .	C	D
I want life to . . . but it doesn't have to . . .	E	F

Figure 3 The 3 × 2 health matrix

The 3 × 2 health matrix

Extrapolating from Dryden et al.'s (1997) 3 × 2 disturbance matrix, it is possible to develop a 3 × 2 health matrix (see Figure 3). I will now discuss the six types of health yielded by this matrix.

(A) Ego health – Non-dogmatic preferences about self

Here, the person concerned holds non-dogmatic preferences concerning herself and the main derivative from this flexible belief is some aspect of self-acceptance, for example:

- "I would like to do well in my exams, but I don't have to do so. If I don't, I can accept myself as a fallible human being who is not doing as well as she likes."
- "I want to be loved and approved by certain people in my life, but I don't have to be. If I am not, that's a shame but it does not prove I'm no good. I am the same person whether I am loved and approved or not."

(B) Discomfort tolerance – Non-dogmatic preferences about self

Here, the person holds non-dogmatic preferences about herself, but the real issue concerns her attitude towards discomfort. For example:

- "If I don't obtain my degree, I might have to settle for some kind of tedious, manual job. I want to achieve more that this, but I don't have to do so. If I don't, it would be a struggle for me to tolerate the hardship, but I could bear it and it would be worth it to me to do so."

(C) Ego health – Non-dogmatic preferences about others

In this example, the person holds non-dogmatic preferences about the behaviour (or its absence) of another, but the real issue centres round her attitude towards herself. For example:

- "If you don't treat me, it means that you don't think much of me. I would like you to think well of me, but you don't have to do so. If you don't, I can still accept myself as a person."

(D) Discomfort tolerance – Non-dogmatic preferences about others

Here, the person holds non-dogmatic preferences about others, but the real issue concerns the realm of discomfort. For example:

- "I want you to treat me nicely, but you don't have to do so. If you don't, it would difficult for me to put up with the hard life I'd be faced with, but I can do so and it is worth it to me to do so."

(E) Ego health – Non-dogmatic preferences about life conditions

On the surface, the person is holding non-dogmatic preferences about some aspects of life conditions, but the real issue concerns her attitude towards herself. For example:

- "I want life conditions under which I live to be easy for me, but it doesn't have to be that way. If they are not easy then that does not prove that I am worthless. I can accept myself whatever life conditions I face."

51

(F) Discomfort tolerance – Non-dogmatic preferences about life conditions

In this final type of health we are dealing with a more impersonal form of high frustration tolerance. For example:

- "I don't want the frustration of my car breaking down when I'm just about to use it, but I don't have to have my desires met. If it did break down, that would be a pain, but I can stand the frustration if it did."
- "When I join a queue for some service, I want to be served quickly, but I don't have to be. Although it is a struggle, I can stand delays in getting what I want and it is worth it to me to do so."

12

Focus on meta-emotional disturbance

While other approaches to CBT do recognise that people disturb themselves about their disturbances, none focus on this phenomenon as much as REBT. The fact that humans disturb themselves about their disturbance has been variously referred to as symptom stress (Walen, DiGiuseppe, & Dryden, 1992), problems about problems and meta-emotional disturbance, which literally means emotional disturbance about emotional disturbance (e.g. Dryden, 2002).

If we consider the concept of meta-emotional disturbance more closely, we find that it has a number of different features.

UNEs at "A"; UNEs at "C"

When we disturb ourselves at "C1" about the adversities in our lives at "A1", we can then focus on these unhealthy negative emotions (UNEs) and disturb ourselves about them. When we do this, these UNEs, which were originally located at "C1", become adversities at "A2" and our disturbed emotional responses to them are located at "C2". This is shown below:

A1 = Original adversity

B1 = Irrational belief

C1 = UNE1

A2 = UNE1

B2 = Irrational belief

C2 = UNE2

Inferences about UNEs at "A"; UNEs at "C"

We not only disturb ourselves about our unhealthy negative emotions when we experience them, we also disturb ourselves about the inferences we make about these emotions. This is shown below:

A1 = Original adversity

B1 = Irrational belief

C1 = UNE 1

A2 = Inference about UNE1

B2 = Irrational belief

C2 = UNE2

For example, let's suppose that I feel anxious about giving a poor public speech. I then make myself anxious about the anxiety that I first experience. Now I can either feel anxious about the feeling of anxiety (which I have just discussed above) or I can feel anxious about my anxiety because I take it that it means that I am losing control which is my inference. Here I am more anxious about losing control than I am about the anxiety itself.

These two different scenarios are shown opposite:

A1 = Doing poorly at public speech

B1 = Irrational belief

C1 = Anxiety

A2 = Feelings of anxiety

B2 = Irrational belief

C2 = Increased anxiety

A1 = Doing poorly at public speech

B1 = Irrational belief

C1 = Anxiety

A2 = Losing control (inference about C1)

B2 = Irrational belief

C2 = Increased anxiety

13

The biological basis of human irrationality

Ellis (1976) has argued that humans have two basic biological tendencies. First, we have a tendency towards irrationality; we naturally tend to make ourselves disturbed. Second, we have a tendency towards becoming aware of our irrationality and towards working steadily towards rationality. Ellis (1976) noted that this second tendency requires more effort than the first!

Ellis (1976) made a number of points in support of this "biological hypothesis". These included the following:

Human irrationality is ubiquitous

Virtually all humans show evidence of major human irrationalities. Thus, virtually all of us disturb ourselves about life's adversities. Of course, we do not disturb ourselves about the same adversities and the extent of our disturbance will vary from person to person, but virtually all of us do this. Our disturbance does not interfere with the survival of the species and most of the time it does not interfere with our individual existence. As Ellis often used to say, "Mother nature is concerned with our survival not with the emotional quality of our life". The latter is firmly within our responsibility and the fact that many of us needlessly disturb ourselves shows that this tendency is rooted in our humanity.

Conversely consider how different our lives would be if human rationality were as ubiquitous as human irrationality appears to be. It would be very difficult for us to disturb ourselves about life's adversities. We would rarely procrastinate and would persist at striving towards our goals. We would be very self-disciplined and would live longer because we would rarely smoke and would tend to keep to healthy eating regimes. This is obviously not the case and although we have the ability to think and act rationally, the fact that we find it hard to sustain doing so is evidence for Ellis's (1976) view that there is a strong biological basis to human irrationality.

Ease in thinking in rigid and extreme ways

Earlier in this book I distinguished between flexible beliefs and non-extreme beliefs, on the one hand and rigid and extreme beliefs on the other. I commented that REBT theory posited that rigid and extreme beliefs are at the core of psychological disturbance and that flexible and non-extreme beliefs are at the core of psychological health. I showed, in particular, that both rigid beliefs and flexible beliefs are very frequently based on our desires, but what distinguishes them is when we hold rigid beliefs we transform these desires into rigid, absolute necessities, but when we hold flexible beliefs we keep our desires flexible and acknowledge to ourselves that we do not have to have our desires met. I also showed that extreme and non-extreme beliefs stem from rigid and flexible beliefs respectively.

Now, REBT theory holds that when our desires are weak then we find it relatively easy to keep our beliefs flexible and non-extreme when our desires are not met. However, when our desires become stronger and particularly when they are very strong, then we find it very much more difficult to retain flexibility and non-extremity in our beliefs. In other words, when our desires are strong, then we find it relatively easy to transform these desires into absolute necessities and the fact that it is bad and tolerable when we don't get what we want into the idea that it is awful and unbearable to be thus thwarted. Again, the ease with which most humans do this points to the biological underpinnings of this common form of human irrationality. If we were strongly biologically prone to retain flexible and non-extreme beliefs in the face of our very strong desires not being met, then we would find it very difficult to think in rigid and extreme ways under these circumstances and would tend not to do so even if strongly encouraged to do so by our culture.

For example, let's suppose that I hold a weak desire about being picked by my college to represent it at a marketing function. If I was not picked, it would be relatively easy for me to retain flexibility and non-extremity in my belief system. I would begin by saying: "It is somewhat important for me to be selected to represent my college . . .", and I would conclude thus, ". . . but I don't have to be chosen and it is bad, but not terrible if I'm not". However, if my desire was very strong I would struggle to retain my flexible and non-extreme belief. Here, I would begin by saying: "It is really important for me to be selected to represent my college . . .", however I would then easily conclude, ". . . and therefore I have to be selected and it would be terrible if I weren't". I would have to work very hard to go back and remain with my flexible and non-extreme beliefs. The fact that I would have to work so hard shows that it is difficult for me as a human to stay with my flexible and non-extreme beliefs when my unmet desires are very strong.

While human irrationality is ubiquitous and the tendency for humans to transform their very strong desires into rigid dire necessities and into extreme views when these desires are not met seems universal, there seems to be a good deal of individual differences in the extent and ease with which people disturb themselves. A few rarely do so and only when their thwarted desires are paramount do they transform these into rigid and extreme beliefs. On the other hand, others seem to transform even very weak desires into rigidities when they don't get what they want. This is particularly the case with people who have a severe personality disorder (Ellis, 2002).

Human irrationality is taught less frequently than human rationality

Many human irrationalities actually go counter to the teachings of parents, peers and the mass media (for example, people are rarely taught that it is good to procrastinate, yet countless do so). Children are frequently told that just because they want something it doesn't mean that they must get it. Yet despite such teachings, countless people procrastinate and we all tend to demand that we have to get what we want in some area or another. If human rationality was biologically based, frequent cultural teachings about the value of anti-procrastination and non-demandingness would have a far greater impact than they seem to.

Humans easily lapse, relapse and replace one irrationality with another

While humans have a tendency to think and act irrationally, they also have a tendency to think about their thinking and behaviour and to work towards greater rationality. If we did not have the potential to be rational, then the efforts of counsellors and therapists would be in vain. However, once we have actualised our tendency to be rational, we often go back to irrational activity even though we have worked hard to overcome it. (Ellis, 1976). Thus, we frequently lapse in our efforts to become and stay rational in certain key areas. For example, we may for a while give up certain self-defeating habits, but then lapse back into these habits for a time when the going gets tough. We may even relapse and end up as irrational as we were when we first began a programme of self-help.

Also, when we are successful at helping ourselves with our irrational thinking in one area, we may well replace this irrationality with another. Thus, some people are able to overcome their irrational thinking about smoking, but then develop irrational ideas about food. It may be that while we keep a disciplined eye in one area of our lives, we let go of such a rational perspective in other areas. A recent beginning of the year ad campaign from Boots the Chemist in Britain urged its customers to make one small change, in recognition of the failure experienced by most people in tackling several areas of poor self-discipline at once!

The ease with which we lapse and relapse, the ease with which we replace one irrationality with another and the great difficulty we have at making several changes at once, all point again to the biological basis of this form of irrationality. As a species, we find it inordinately difficult to think and act rationally in the first place and to acquire and, particularly, maintain rational thinking and action in the second place.

14

Choice-based constructivism and going against the grain

While there are a number of constructivistic approaches to CBT (see Dobson, 2001), REBT's position on the issue of constructivism is distinctive in that it emphasises that we create or construct our rigid and extreme ideas from our preferences. I have already argued above that this constructivistic tendency is biologically based. What is important to factor in here is the point that I have already made; namely, that we also have a biologically-based tendency to think rationally about life's adversities.

As such, we have a choice: we can choose to construct rigid and extreme ideas from our desires or we can choose to construct and remain with flexible and non-extreme ideas in relation to our desires. I have argued that we find it very easy to transform our desires into absolute necessities when these desires are strong and have a tough time being flexible about the attainment of these desires. This point also applies about the ease with which we construct extreme ideas when our desires are thwarted and the difficulty we have in constructing and remaining with non-extreme ideas when our desires are unmet. However difficult we find it being rational (i.e. thinking flexibly and in non-extreme ways) in the face of life's adversities and/or when our strong desires are not met, REBT theory says that we can choose to construct and remain with rational ideas under these circumstances even though it goes against the grain for us to do so. This means that we can choose to think rationally even though we have a strong tendency to choose to construct and remain with irrational (i.e. rigid and extreme) ideas. This "going against the grain" thinking is difficult to sustain without commitment, force and energy and a determination to align one's behaviour and inferential thinking with rational beliefs, and a corresponding determination not to act and think in ways that may perpetuate our irrational beliefs. The idea that we can with great effort think and act rationally under very difficult circumstances is a hallmark of REBT.

15

Position on good mental health

In the US TV series, at the end of his radio programme, Frasier wishes the people of Seattle "good mental health". However, he never outlines what this is. REBT, on the other hand, is very explicit about what constitutes good mental health, more explicit in this respect than other CBT therapies. REBT not only sees its aim as the remediation of psychological disturbance, it also strives to help clients to work towards being as psychologically healthy as possible. This is how REBT conceptualises good mental health:

Personal responsibility

People with good mental health (GMH) accept full responsibility for their emotional disturbances and will strive to overcome their own emotional and behavioural problems by utilising the methods and techniques of REBT and CBT. They acknowledge that situations and other people contribute to their disturbance, but they resist the temptation to blame their feelings on these situations/people.

Flexibility and anti-extremism

People with GMH have a belief system made up largely of flexible and non-extreme beliefs. When they do disturb themselves by holding rigid and extreme beliefs they recognise this and take steps as soon as they can to question these beliefs and to hold and act on the flexible and non-extreme alternatives to these beliefs.

As we have seen, people with GMH have desires but don't transform them into demands on self, others and life conditions. They acknowledge badness, but don't awfulise, they tolerate frustration and discomfort when it is in their healthy interests to do so, and they accept themselves and others as fallible human beings and life as a complex mixture of the good, the bad and the neutral.

By definition such people are open to change and are minimally defensive.

Scientific thinking and non-Utopian in outlook

People with GMH tend to be scientific in their thinking. They tend to regulate their emotions and actions by reflecting on them and evaluating their consequences in terms of the extent to which they lead to the attainment of their short-term and long-term goals. They also see their inferences as hunches about reality rather than facts, and are prepared to examine their accuracy by looking at the available evidence.

They are also sceptical and don't accept as true assertions that appear attractive or because an authority states that they are true. They have an independent mind.

Finally, they accept the fact that Utopias are probably unachievable and also recognise that it is unlikely that they will get everything they want and that they will frequently experience frustration in their lives.

Enlightened self-interest

People with GMH tend to be first and primarily interested in themselves and to put their own healthy interests at least a little above the interests of others. However, they sacrifice themselves to some degree for those for whom they care but not overwhelmingly or completely. They also show themselves as much compassion and caring as they do the significant others in their life.

Social interest

People with GMH also realise that if they do not act morally to protect the rights of others and abet social survival, it is unlikely that they will help to create the kind of world in which they themselves can live comfortably and happily.

Self-direction

Because people with GMH take responsibility for their lives they are largely self-directing while simultaneously preferring to co-operate with others. In doing so, they do not *need* the support or help of others although they regard these as being desirable. They are not proud to ask for help when they need to and do not regard themselves as weak for doing so.

High tolerance of uncertainty

People with GMH have a high tolerance for uncertainty and do not demand that they must know what is going to happen to them or to others. As such they do not act impulsively or seek reassurance when it is not appropriate to do so.

Strong commitment to meaningful pursuits

People with GMH realise that they tend to be healthier and happier when they are vitally absorbed in something outside of themselves. REBT does not have anything relevant to say about what these meaningful pursuits should be as there is an enormous range of such activities available to people. In this area, it encourages people to be themselves and go for what they find meaningful no matter how strange this may appear to others, although it also encourages others to be mindful of the reactions of others (see the section on social interest above).

Calculated risk taking

People with GMH tend to take a fair number of risks and try to do what they want to do even where there's a good chance that they might fail. They tend to be adventurous but not foolhardy in this respect and act on the maxim: nothing ventured, nothing gained, or as my mother used to say, "If you don't ask, you don't get!"

Long-range hedonism

People with GMH are willing to forgo short-term pleasures when these interfere with the pursuit of their long-term constructive goals. In this respect they have a philosophy of high frustration tolerance by showing that they do not have to get what they want immediately and can unrebelliously buckle down to doing necessary but boring tasks when it is in their best interests to do so promptly.

REBT, however, is no killjoy therapy. It also believes that people with GMH are passionate individuals who like to enjoy themselves. Thus, REBT encourages people to go for immediate pleasure when doing so has no adverse long-term implications.

Part 2

THE DISTINCTIVE PRACTICAL FEATURES OF REBT

16

The therapeutic relationship in REBT

The consensus view in the cognitive-behaviour therapies is that the core conditions outlined many years ago by Carl Rogers (1957) – namely, empathy, respect and genuineness – are solid foundations for therapeutic change, but are neither necessary nor sufficient for change to occur. REBT concurs with this view, but also outlines some distinct contributions to the therapeutic relationship that will be the focus of the present discussion.

Therapist warmth

Ellis (in Dryden, 1997) has argued that while most other therapeutic approaches encourage therapists to be warm towards their clients, REBT advocates therapists giving unconditional acceptance rather than giving warmth or approval to clients. Other cognitive-behavioural approaches to therapy tend not to make this distinction. Ellis holds that therapist warmth and approval have their distinct dangers in that they may unwittingly encourage clients to strengthen their dire needs for love and approval.

Therapist acceptance

In his original formulation, Rogers (1957) argued that it is an important therapeutic ingredient for therapists to be experienced by their clients as showing them positive regard for them. This concept of positive regard has also been referred to by person-centred therapists as "prizing" and "respect". What unites these concepts is that the therapists convey that they

regard clients as persons of worth and that they do this unconditionally. You will see that this is akin to the concept of
unconditional worth discussed in Point 10. Other CBT therapists would concur with this idea of therapists showing clients
unconditional respect.

While REBT therapists would not disagree with this idea, we
prefer showing our clients that we unconditionally accept them
as fallible human beings who are neither worthwhile nor
worthless since they are far too complex to be given a single
evaluation and in any respect are constantly in flux, which
would soon render such single ratings out of date even if they
were legitimate, which they are not. This stance is consistent
with REBT's position on human worth, which I discussed in
Point 10.

Informality

REBT therapists tend towards informality of therapeutic style
although we can be formal when required. This informality
communicates a number of messages to clients. First, it says
that REBT therapists take themselves and their role seriously,
but not too seriously. Second, informality tends to lessen the
emotional distance between therapist and client without losing
sight of the fact that this relationship has been established
to help the client to achieve their therapeutic goals. Third, it
tends to communicate therapeutic parity between therapist
and client.

Actually, REBT's position on parity in therapy is as follows.
When it comes to the business of conceptualising clients' problems and effecting change in these problems, REBT therapists
are decidedly superior to their clients . . . or at least (ideally)
should be. However, when it comes to their value as human
beings, then REBT's position is that they are equivalent in
value because they are both, fallible, ever-changing human
beings far too complex to merit a single rating such as value
or worth!

Humour

There is a consensus view in REBT that therapist humour is an effective part of the therapeutic relationship between therapist and client. Certainly therapist humour is emphasised more heavily in REBT than in other CBT approaches. Therapist humour should be focused on aspects of clients rather than directed at the clients themselves and should have the quality of laughing with clients rather than laughing at clients. The use of humour in REBT stems from Ellis's (1987) view that one way of looking at psychological disturbance is that it occurs when people take themselves, other people and/or life conditions not just seriously, but *too* seriously. Therapist humour is effective when it encourages clients to stand back and see the ridiculous in their thinking and behaviour and when it promotes a determination to think and act rationally. As with other interventions, REBT therapists should not use humour with all clients, and it is worth noting in passing that not all REBT therapists have the capacity to use humour effectively in therapy.

17

Position on case formulation

Persons (1989), in a seminal book, highlighted the importance of adopting a case-formulation (sometimes called case-conceptualisation) approach to the practice of CBT. A case formulation is essentially a blueprint, which takes as its starting point a client's presenting problems and puts forward hypotheses about factors that account for these problems and explain how the client unwittingly perpetuates these problems. These factors are mainly cognitive and behavioural, but environmental and interpersonal context factors are also included.

A good case formulation also considers the relationships between a client's problems and possible obstacles to progress and suggests a pragmatic order in which to tackle the person's problems. In short, it provides order to the conceptualisation and treatment of the client's problems.

Currently, most CBT therapists carry out a formulation of a "case" before embarking on treatment unless the need is pressing to treat a client before such a formulation is undertaken. When case formulation is carried out in CBT it is done so collaboratively.

As I discussed in Point 3, REBT therapists use an ABC framework to help ourselves and our clients understand the cognitive-behavioural dynamics of the clients' target problems. This also happens in CBT although what factors are included in a CBT-based ABC assessment may differ in several respects to one carried out in REBT. What we do not routinely do is to wait to intervene on our clients' problems until we have carried out a case formulation. Thus, REBT therapists tend to intervene more quickly on a client's target problem and build up a formulation of the "case" as they go rather than structuring therapy into formulation–intervention stages.

As with many other issues, Ellis is the driving force here. When he started his career he became dissatisfied with an approach to therapy that saw therapeutic intervention being dependent upon a thorough assessment of clients' psycho-pathology and personality based on the completion and analysis of a large number of questionnaires, inventories and other assessment tools. Ellis (1962) regarded this process as inefficient and noted that a significant number of clients tended to drop out of this process before treatment had commenced. Ellis noted the waste of therapist, client and an organisation's time when many person hours were spent on preparing the client for an intervention based on the accumulation and analysis of these data that was subsequently not made because the client had dropped out before treatment proper had com-menced. The legacy of this experience was that Ellis considered it to be the best use of everyone's time and resources if treat-ment was gotten underway as quickly as possible. Hence, Ellis tended to eschew a case-formulation approach to REBT, where a formal formulation routinely precedes treatment. Of course, Ellis was a highly skilled formulator of "cases", as anyone who had received clinical supervision from him will testify. But he tended to do this in his head rather than on paper and, as noted above, he made his formulations during therapy rather than before therapy had gotten underway. Indeed, Ellis argued that a client's response to therapy tells the therapist a great deal about the client and their problems and for this to become manifest, therapy must be initiated.

So, what have other REBT therapists had to say about the use of case formulation in REBT? I have perhaps put forward the most developed approach to the use of a case formulation in REBT (Dryden, 1998). I call this approach UPCP, which stands for "Understanding the Person in the Context of his or her Problems" because I dislike referring to a person as a "case".

I argue that there are number of factors that need to be identified when conducting a UPCP:

1 Basic information on the client and any striking initial impressions.
2 A list of the client's problems.
3 The client's goals for change.
4 A list of the client's problem emotions (UNEs).
5 A list of the client's problem critical "A"s (e.g. disapproval, uncertainty, failure, injustice).
6 The client's core irrational (rigid and extreme) beliefs.
7 A list of the client's dysfunctional behaviours.
8 The purposive nature of dysfunctional behaviour.
9 A list of the ways in which the client prevents or cuts short the experience of their problems.
10 A list of the ways in which the client compensates for problems.
11 A list of meta-emotional problems (see Point 12), pp. 53–55.
12 A list of the cognitive consequences of core irrational beliefs.
13 How the client expresses problems and the interpersonal responses to these expressions.
14 The client's health and medication status.
15 A list of relevant predisposing factors.
16 Predicting the client's likely responses to therapy.

As you can see from the above, developing a UPCP takes time and this time may be better spent in helping the client to address their problems. Thus, I do not recommend that REBT therapists carry out a full UPCP with every client. But it should be conducted:

• When it is clear that the person has many complex problems.
• When resistance occurs in clients who have at first sight non-complex problems and where usual ways of addressing such resistance have proven unsuccessful.
• When clients have had several unsuccessful previous attempts at therapy, particularly REBT.

18

Psycho-educational emphasis

Ellis and Dryden (1997) argued that REBT can usefully be viewed as a psycho-educational approach to therapy. In this respect, REBT has a decided view of the nature of psychological disturbance and how this can be addressed and many of its practitioners largely hold the view that both can be actively taught to clients. Such teaching occurs in all the major therapeutic arenas (individual, couple, family, group) as well as contexts that may be less associated with therapy: workshops for the public and 9 hour intensives (Ellis & Dryden, 1997).

What do we teach our clients in REBT?

In REBT, we teach our clients a range of issues. For example:

1   We teach them at the outset about the essence of REBT and about what they can realistically expect from their therapist and what their therapist can realistically expect from them. Thus we teach them:
    * that life's adversities do not disturb them. Rather, they disturb themselves about life's adversities;
    * that they disturb themselves because they hold irrational (i.e. rigid and extreme) beliefs about life's adversities;
    * what tasks their therapists are likely to carry out in therapy; and
    * what tasks they will in all likelihood be called upon to carry out in the process.

Once we have taught them the above they are in a position to give (or withhold) their informed consent to proceed as a client in REBT.

2   We teach them the dynamics of unhealthy negative emo-
     tions. We show them that each disturbed emotion has
     typical inferences at "A", rigid and extreme beliefs at "B"
     and recurring behaviours and thinking consequences at
     "C".
3   We teach them how to identify their problems and set
     realistic, achievable goals for each of these problems.
4   We teach them to select a target problem at a given point in
     time and to assess this problem accurately using the ABC
     framework (see Point 3 in this book).
5   We teach them to identify any secondary meta-emotional
     problems that they may have and to decide whether or not
     it is better for them to target this problem before their
     primary problem.
6   We teach them that in order for them to un-disturb them-
     selves about life's adversities in general and about the
     adversity they are focusing on in particular, they need to
     change their beliefs about these adversities from irrational
     (i.e. rigid and extreme) to rational (i.e. flexible and non-
     extreme).
7   We teach them that in order for them to change their
     irrational beliefs to rational beliefs they first need to ask
     questions that are targeted at the empirical, logical and
     pragmatic status of these beliefs. In doing so, we teach
     them how to frame such questions to get the most out of
     this process. They are advised to do this until they can see
     why their irrational beliefs are irrational and why their
     rational beliefs are rational. When they reach this stage
     they are said to have achieved intellectual insight into the
     irrationality of their irrational belief and into the ration-
     ality of their rational beliefs. Such insight is the foundation
     of change but does not in itself promote it. Here clients
     typically say: "I understand it in my head, but not in
     my gut".
8   We teach them that once they have achieved intellectual
     insight they have to use a variety of methods to facilitate

emotional insight. It is this insight that leads to clients changing their feelings. We also train them how to use these techniques.

9 We teach clients how they unwittingly perpetuate their problems and what they need to do to break the perpetuation cycle.

10 Once they have made progress, we teach clients what they need to do to minimise the chances of lapsing and relapsing.

11 We teach them how to generalise their learning from one problem to another and later in therapy we teach them what they need to do to become their own therapists.

How is this teaching delivered?

REBT therapists agree with their cognitive therapy colleagues that it is best for clients to be helped to discover for themselves how they disturb themselves cognitively and how they can stand back and question these disturbance-creating cognitions. It is best because self-discovery and the independent thinking that underpins it is an important criterion of good mental health (GMH) – see Point 15. In this regard, both CT and REBT therapists employ Socratic questions to help their clients in this regard. In Socratic questioning, therapists ask their clients open-ended questions and guide them to discover which cognitions are at the root of their problems and how to evaluate and change them. It does not involve therapists didactically telling clients why their cognitions are problematic and how to change them. While REBT therapists favour Socratic methods of teaching in that they encourage independent thinking, we accept that at times we will also have to be didactic when clients do not understand a point through Socratic enquiry. We also acknowledge that some clients do not respond at all well to Socratic methods of teaching but do respond much better to didactic methods and consequently we are quite prepared to work didactically with such clients, more so than our cognitive therapy colleagues. Flexibility of teaching approach is valued, tailoring the teaching method to the client.

Some REBT therapists argue that their prime role is not to help clients to address their emotional problems, but to teach clients to become proficient at using REBT change-based methods so they can address their own emotional problems. To this end these latter REBT therapists use materials to facilitate skill development (e.g. Dryden, 2001).

19

Dealing with problems in order: (i) Disturbance; (ii) Dissatisfaction; (iii) Development

Clients come to REBT with a variety of problems: (i) emotional problems; (ii) practical, dissatisfaction problems; and (iii) personal development problems. A distinctive feature of REBT is that it outlines a logical order for dealing with these problems.

Disturbance before dissatisfaction

REBT argues that unless there are good reasons to the contrary, it is best to help clients address their emotional problems before their dissatisfaction problems. The reasoning is as follows. If clients try and deal with their dissatisfaction before they deal with their emotional disturbance, then their disturbed feelings will get in the way of their efforts to change directly the negative "A"s about which they are dissatisfied.

For example, let's take the example of Paul who is dissatisfied about his wife's spending habits. However, he is also unhealthily angry about her behaviour and every time he talks to her about it he makes himself angry about it, raises his voice to his wife and makes pejorative remarks about her and her spending behaviour. Now what is the likely impact of Paul's expression of unhealthy anger on his wife? Does it encourage her to stand back and look objectively at her own behaviour? Of course it doesn't. Paul's angry behaviour is more likely to lead his wife to become unhealthily angry herself and/or to become defensive. In Paul's case, his anger had, in fact, both effects on his wife. Now, lets suppose that Paul *first* addressed his unhealthy anger and then discussed his dissatisfaction with his wife. His annoyance at her behaviour, but his acceptance of her as a person would help him to view her behaviour perhaps as a sign of emotional disturbance and his compassion for her would have very different effects on her. She would probably be less defensive and because Paul would not be unhealthily angry, then his wife would also be less likely to be unhealthily angry. With anger out of the picture, the stage would be set for Paul to address the reasons for his dissatisfaction more effectively.

Disturbance before development

In the late 1960s and early 1970s, I used to go to a number of encounter groups. This was the era of personal growth or development. However, there were a number of casualties of these groups and when these occurred it was because attendees were preoccupied with issues of emotional disturbance and they were being pushed too hard to go into areas of development that warranted greater resilience.

In general, then, it is very difficult for clients to develop themselves when they are emotionally disturbed. To focus on areas of development when someone is emotionally disturbed is akin to encouraging that person to climb a very steep hill with very heavy weights attached to their ankles. First, help the person to remove their ankle weights (i.e. address their emotional disturbance) before discussing the best way of climbing the hill!

Dissatisfaction before development

Abraham Maslow (1968) is perhaps best known for his work on self-actualisation. The relevance of this concept for our present discussion is this. It is very difficult for humans to focus on higher-order "needs" when they are preoccupied with issues with respect to lower-order needs. Thus, if a client is faced with a general dissatisfying life experience, which cannot be compartmentalised, and also wants to explore his writing ambitions, help him with the former first unless this life dissatisfaction will help him write a better book!

While I have outlined REBT's preferred order in dealing with problems, don't forget that it values flexibility. Thus, if clients want to deal with their problems in a different order and maintain this position even after their REBT therapists have given their rationale for the disturbance–dissatisfaction–development order then their wishes should be accommodated. In all probability, their resultant experiences will testify to REBT's position!!

20

Early focus on iBs

Most approaches within the CBT tradition argue that cognitions occur at different levels in our cognitive system. Thus, cognitive therapists hold that automatic thoughts (often in the form of inferences) occur at the surface of our cognitive system, styles of information processing occur in the middle range of this system and cognitive schemata occur more centrally within it. In this framework, irrational beliefs can be regarded as a form of cognitive schemata in that they are beliefs rather than inferences or information processing styles. While most approaches to CBT begin at the more surface levels of the cognitive system, REBT is distinct in that it recommends that therapists encourage clients as quickly as possible to focus on the irrational, rigid and extreme beliefs that underpin their disturbed reactions, unless there are good reasons not to do so. As such, REBT adopts a hypothetico-deductive approach to assessment (DiGiuseppe, 1991a)

The rationale for this early focus on iBs is as follows. According to REBT theory rigid and extreme irrational beliefs are at the core of clients' emotional problems. Therefore, if clients are to be helped to address these problems effectively they need to identify and change these irrational beliefs to their flexible and non-extreme rational alternatives. This is best and most efficiently done by a direct focus on these beliefs unless, as I said above, there are good reasons not to do this.

What this means in practice is that the REBT therapist will encourage the client to select a specific problem on which to focus. The therapist will then ask the client to select a specific example of this problem. This specific example will then be the focus for assessment using REBT's ABC framework discussed earlier (see Point 3). During this assessment, the client will be encouraged to assume temporarily that their "A" is true so that the therapist can help them to identify and work with their irrational beliefs. Other therapists in the cognitive-behavioural tradition are more likely to deal with distorted inferences (which occur at "A" in REBT's ABC framework) or with their errors in information processing early on in therapy.

21

Helping clients to change their irrational beliefs to rational beliefs

Perhaps the most distinctive feature about REBT practice is the efforts that REBT therapists make to help our clients change their irrational (rigid and extreme) beliefs to rational (flexible and non-extreme) beliefs. This process involves a number of steps.

Helping clients to detect their irrational beliefs

The first step in helping clients to change their irrational beliefs to their rational alternatives is to assist them to detect their irrational beliefs. In the first instance this involves teaching clients about irrational beliefs and their nature. As we saw in Points 4 and 6, irrational beliefs are characterised by rigidity and by being extreme. Rigid beliefs occur most frequently in the form of demands and musts and extreme beliefs, which are derived from these rigid beliefs take the form of awfulising beliefs, low frustration tolerance (LFT) beliefs and depreciation (of self, others and life conditions) beliefs. REBT therapists use a number of ways to teach clients about this vital aspect of REBT theory and help them to apply this knowledge in the assessment process to detect the irrational beliefs that underpin their emotional problems.

Helping clients to discriminate their irrational beliefs from their rational belief alternatives

REBT theory holds that if REBT therapists are going to help their clients overcome their problems most effectively, then they need to help them to think rationally about life's adversities rather than irrationally. As part of this process, an important task is helping clients to discriminate their irrational beliefs from their rational beliefs. In the same way that we educate our clients to understand what irrational beliefs are and the forms that they take we also teach them to understand what rational beliefs are and the forms that they take.

A very important part of this process is helping clients to understand keenly the differences between irrational beliefs and rational beliefs.

For example, it is not sufficient to show a client that the rational alternative to her (in this case) rigid belief, "I must impress my new boss straightaway" is the belief: "I'd like to impress my boss straightaway". The latter may not be rigid, but it is not fully flexible. While it asserts her preference, it does not negate her demand. The flexible belief alternative to her rigid belief is: "I'd like to impress my new boss straightaway, but I do not have to do so", which incorporates both components of the flexible beliefs (see Point 5).

Table 1 outlines clearly the full differences between rigid and extreme beliefs on the one hand and flexible and non-extreme beliefs on the other.

Disputing clients' irrational and rational beliefs

After we have helped our clients to see the differences between their rational and irrational beliefs, REBT therapists move on to disputing these beliefs with them. This is done after clients understand the relationship between their irrational beliefs and their emotional problems and their rational beliefs and their goals.

As DiGiuseppe (1991b) has shown, disputing involves questioning *both* clients' irrational *and* rational beliefs to the point where they see the reasons for the irrationality of the former (i.e. they are false, illogical and lead largely to poor results) and for the rationality of the latter (i.e. they are true, logical and

Table 1 Irrational and rational beliefs in REBT theory

Irrational belief	Rational belief
Demand X must (or must not happen)	*Non-dogmatic preference* I would like X to happen (or not happen), but it does not have to be the way I want it to be
Awfulising belief It would be terrible if X happens (or does not happen)	*Anti-awfulising belief* It would be bad, but not terrible, if X happens (or does not happen)
LFT belief I could not bear it if X happens (or does not happen)	*HFT belief* It would be difficult to bear if X happens (or does not happen), but I could bear it and it would be worth it to me to do so
Depreciation belief If X happens (or does not happen) I am no good/you are no good/life is no good	*Acceptance belief* If X happens (or does not happen), it does not prove that I am no good/you are no good/life is no good. Rather, I am a FHB/you are a FHB, life is a complex/mixture of good bad and neutral

Notes: FHB = Fallible human being; LFT = Low frustration tolerance; HFT = High frustration tolerance.

lead largely to good results). In addition, short didactic explanations are given until clients reach the same insight. These questions/explanations are directed to clients' rigid and flexible beliefs as well as to their extreme and non-extreme beliefs and this is done using a variety of styles (see Point 23).

In this context a distinctive feature of REBT is its emphasis on strong disputing with certain clients at certain times in the therapeutic process, particularly when clients are demonstrating resistance (Ellis, 2002). This contrasts with cognitive therapy, the founder of which has recently argued that cognitive therapists should not challenge their clients' dysfunctional beliefs because to do so sounds confrontational. Rather they should help their clients examine, evaluate or test such beliefs, a far more gentle enterprise than disputing and certainly than strong disputing (Beck, 2002).

22

Use of logical arguments in disputing beliefs

In common with other CBT therapists, REBT therapists ask clients questions about the empirical status and the pragmatic status of their beliefs. However, we also ask them about the logical status of their beliefs, which other CBT therapists do less frequently. It may be that empirical and pragmatic arguments are more persuasive to clients than logical arguments. We do not know because the relevant research has not been done. Even if this is the case, in general, REBT therapists would still use logical disputing of beliefs for two reasons. First, we do not know on a priori grounds which clients will find which arguments most persuasive in changing their irrational beliefs to their rational alternatives. Just because the majority of clients may find logical arguments unpersuasive, it does not follow that all will do so and to withhold such arguments from those who might find them persuasive would not be good practice. So, REBT therapists tend to use all three arguments to see, as I said above, which arguments will be most persuasive with which clients.

Also, we use empirical, pragmatic *and* logical arguments while disputing beliefs in order to be comprehensive. This comprehensiveness may itself be effective. Thus, even if clients find empirical and pragmatic arguments more persuasive than logical arguments, it may still be worthwhile employing such arguments in that they may add value to the overall effectiveness of the disputing process. Some clients may find it persuasive that their irrational beliefs are false, unhealthy *and* logical even if they find the logical argument weak on its own.

Using logical disputing in action

Since logical disputing of beliefs is a distinctive feature of REBT practice, let's see how it is used in clinical practice.

Having identified your client's rigid demand and non-dogmatic preference ask her (in this case): "Which is logical and which is illogical and why?"

Your client needs to acknowledge that her demand is illogical while her non-dogmatic preference is logical. Help her to see that her demand is based on the same desire as her non-dogmatic preference, but that she transforms it as follows:

I prefer that X happens (or does not happen) . . . and therefore this absolutely must (or must not) happen.

Show her that this belief has two components. The first [I prefer that X happens (or does not happen)] is not rigid, but the second [. . . and therefore this must (or must not) happen] is rigid. As such her rigid demand isn't logical since one cannot logically derive something rigid from something that is not rigid. Use the template in Figure 4 with your client to illustrate this visually, if necessary.

Your client's non-dogmatic preference is as follows:

I prefer that X happens (or does not happen) . . . but this does not mean that it must (or must not) happen.

Her non-dogmatic preference is logical since both parts are not rigid and thus the second component logically follows from the first. Again, use the template in Figure 4 with your client to illustrate this visually, if necessary.

If your client gives you any other answer then help her through discussion to see why her answer is incorrect and help her to accept the correct answer.

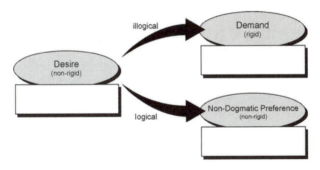

Figure 4 Template for the logical disputing of demands and non-dogmatic preferences

An example of Ellis using logical arguments in therapy

In this segment Ellis (in Dryden, 2002) is disputing the irrational beliefs of a client who insists that because he (in this case) treated his friend very nicely and fairly, this friend *absolutely should* treat him the same way. He does so using primarily logical arguments.

Ellis: Let's suppose that you're describing the situation with your friend accurately and that he treats you shabbily and unfairly after you consistently treat him well. How does it follow that because of your good behaviour he has to respond in kind?

Client: But he's unfair if he doesn't!

Ellis: Yes, we're agreeing on that. He *is* unfair and you are fair. Can you jump from "Because I'm very fair to him, he *has to be* fair to me?"

Client: But he's wrong if he isn't fair when I am.

Ellis: Agreed. But because you are fair, and presumably right, and because he takes advantage of your fairness, does it *still* follow that he has to be right and to treat you fairly?

Client: It logically follows.

Ellis: Does it? It looks like a complete non sequitur to me.

Client: How so?

Ellis: Well, it's logical or consistent that he preferably should treat you fairly when you treat him well. But aren't you making an illogical – or "magical" – jump from "Because he *preferably* should treat me fairly" to "he *absolutely has to* do so?" What "logical" law of the universe leads to your "He absolutely has to do so?"

Client: No law, I guess.

Ellis: No, in logic we get necessitous conclusions, such as, "If all men are human and John must be a man, John must be human". But your "logic" says, "People who get treated fairly, often treat others fairly; I treat my friend fairly; therefore it is absolutely *necessary* that he treat me similarly". Is that a logical conclusion?

Client: I guess not.

Ellis: Moreover, you seem to be claiming that because you act fairly and your friend behaves unfairly, his *acts* make him a *rotten person*. Is that logical thinking?

Client: Why not?

Ellis: It's illogical because you're over-generalising. You're jumping from one of his rotten *behaviours* – or even one of his *traits* – to categorising HIM, his totality as "rotten". How does that over-generalisation follow from a few of his behaviours?

Client: I can see now that it doesn't.

Ellis: So, what could you more logically conclude instead? [Here Ellis encourages the client to be active in his thinking.]

Client: Well, I could think that he is an equal to one of his main behaviours. He is a person who often, but not always, acts rottenly.

Ellis: Good! Alfred Korzybski and his followers in General Semantics would approve of your new conclusion!

23

Variety of therapeutic styles

Cognitive therapists are advised to adopt a therapeutic style based on the principles of collaborative empiricism (e.g. Beck, Rush, Shaw, & Emery, 1979). This advocates therapist and client working together as equal partners in pursuit of cognitive accuracy and realism through the identification and examining of unrealistic, biased cognitions. REBT therapists would not take issue with this. How we tend to differ from other cognitive-behaviour therapists is that we are prepared to adopt a broader range of therapeutic styles than they tend to use. For example, in 1981, I spent a six-month sabbatical at the then Center for Cognitive Therapy in Philadelphia learning cognitive therapy. As part of our training we had to present our work with a patient in a case conference setting and demonstrate our work with video excerpts. I presented my work with a patient with whom I had a good rapport and used humour as a way of helping her (in this case) to re-evaluate her faulty cognitions, which in her case was very effective. Virtually the entire case conference was devoted to a discussion of how I could have worked more according to the principles of collaborative empiricism and how I could have used non-humorous interventions to achieve similar ends.

I think that this was one of the factors that led me away from cognitive therapy and re-affirmed my commitment to REBT. REBT theory was broad enough to incorporate a number of therapeutic styles and enabled me to practise effective therapy while expressing the different sides of my personality. This was also a major reason why I did not pursue my initial training in person-centred therapy and psychodynamic therapy. My view was that both of these approaches constrained my personality so that I could not practise each mode genuinely.

REBT, by contrast, is not prescriptive in its advice on how REBT is practised, other than the therapist needs to be active–directive, which is the case in virtually all CBT approaches. To demonstrate REBT's flexibility with respect to therapeutic style, consider DiGiuseppe's (1991b) analysis of different styles in cognitively disputing irrational beliefs. He shows that irrational beliefs can be disputed in four styles: Socratically, didactically, metaphorically and humorously. I have added a fifth style, which is disputing irrational beliefs enactively. Let me briefly discuss them.

- *Socratic style*. As discussed in Point 21, here REBT therapists ask their clients open-ended questions designed to encourage them to see that their irrational beliefs are irrational and that rational beliefs are rational and the reasons why this is the case.
- *Didactic style*. Here REBT therapists didactically teach clients the same thing, ensuring that clients understand the didactic points being made.
- *Metaphorical style*. Here REBT therapists adopt a metaphorical stance and tell stories designed to illustrate the irrationality of irrational beliefs and the rationality of rational beliefs. However, unlike indirect approaches to the use of metaphor in therapy, REBT advocates that its practitioners ensure that their clients understand the points being made metaphorically.
- *Humorous style*. Here, REBT therapists use humour to encourage clients to see how ridiculous their irrational ideas are.
- *Enactive style*. Here, REBT therapists use action in the therapy setting to illustrate the irrationality of irrational ideas. For example, to demonstrate the irrationality of depreciating oneself on the basis of one's action, I sometimes throw a glass of water over myself in the therapy

session and ask my client whether that was a stupid thing to do (arguably yes) and am I a stupid person for acting stupidly (rationally no). It is unlikely that many cognitive therapists would use enactive techniques as an everyday part of their therapeutic armamentarium.

Arnold Lazarus (1981) has written on effective therapists being like authentic chameleons. This means that therapists are prepared to, and have the interpersonal flexibility to, modify, with authenticity, their therapeutic style according to the perceived needs of their clients. REBT would very much agree with Lazarus on this point.

24

Discourages gradualism

Another distinctive feature of REBT is its stance on the speed with which clients should ideally face adverse situations and practise thinking rationally in these situations. Many years ago, Joseph Wolpe (1958) developed a therapeutic technique, called systematic desensitisation, based on the principle of reciprocal inhibition. Focusing on anxiety, Wolpe argued that the best way of dealing with anxiety was to inhibit the anxiety response to a threat by replacing that response with one that was incompatible with anxiety; namely, a relaxation response. In order to do this, Wolpe argued that the therapist had to work very gradually up a sophisticated hierarchy of graded anxiety-provoking situations. In doing so, the client was to imagine each situation from a state of relaxation. At the first sign of anxiety, the client was to stop imagining the anxiety-provoking situation and return to the relaxation state before returning to imagining the anxious scene. When the client could do this, they would then take one step up the hierarchy and repeat the procedure. Therapist and client would work very gradually up the hierarchy until the client could imagine the most anxiety-provoking scene in a state of relaxation.

Ellis (1983b) argued against the use of gradualism in the treatment of anxiety and other psychological disorders. He argued instead that clients should be encouraged to face their fears as implosively as they could tolerate while practising thinking rationally in such situations. His argument was threefold.

First, a gradual approach to therapeutic change is not cost effective in terms of treatment sessions. It takes a very long time to help clients to work their way up hierarchies, particularly where these are complex and contain a lot of items.

Second, the process does not encourage client self-reliance. The process is normally heavily dependent on the presence of the therapist, although latterly more automated desensitisation programmes were developed.

Third, and perhaps most crucially, a very gradual approach to the treatment of anxiety and other psychological disorders unwittingly has two main, related side-effects:

1   First, gradualism reinforces clients' philosophy of low frustration tolerance. It implicitly teaches them that they must avoid feeling anxious or must only experience low levels of anxiety. They, then, may develop anxiety about anxiety and avoid situations in which they may feel anxious.
2   Second, gradualism may wittingly encourage clients to view themselves as fragile, too weak to cope with anything that is stressful.

REBT tends to favour full exposure in vivo where clients practise thinking rationally while facing what they truly fear. If clients do this then they can make a lot of progress quite quickly. However, many clients will not do this, at least initially, and therefore REBT therapists need to encourage them to proceed according to a principle that I call "challenging, but not overwhelming" (Dryden, 1985) rather than falling back on the gradualism principle. Using the "challenging, but not overwhelming" principle, once therapists have ascertained that their clients are not prepared to use the full exposure principle, they ask them if they are prepared to use rational thinking while facing situations that are challenging for them to face but not currently overwhelming for them. It can be seen that the "challenging, but not overwhelming" principle is a flexible, pragmatic alternative to the "full exposure" and "gradualism" principles.

25

Change is hard work and the use of therapist force and energy

Here is a typical exchange that I have with my clients about psychotherapeutic change:

Windy: Would you like to get over your problems quickly, at a moderate pace or slowly?

Client: Quickly.

Windy: How much effort do you want to put into therapy: a lot, a moderate amount or hardly any. Be honest now?

Client: Well, if I'm honest, hardly any!

Windy: So, let me sum up. You want to get over your problems quickly and with hardly any effort on your part. Is that correct?

Client: Well . . . yes . . . but put like that I guess it's unrealistic.

Windy: Why do you say that?

Client: Because saying that I can get over my problems, which I have had for a long time, quickly and without hardly any effort sounds like magic.

REBT has a very realistic view of psychotherapeutic change. It argues that while clients may ideally want to get over their problems quickly and without making much effort in the process, in reality such change involves much hard work and the speed of change is related to the degree of work put in by the clients.

The reasons why change does involve hard work are as follows:

- Clients often have a strong biologically-based tendency to think irrationally and to hold their rigid and extreme beliefs very strongly (see Point 13). As a result, effort and force is often needed to change such strongly held beliefs.
- Clients have often had much practice at holding their rigid and extreme beliefs and thus they have often become "second nature" to them.
- Clients often act and think in ways that are consistent with their irrational beliefs. This means that if they are going to change their irrational beliefs to rational beliefs, they need to act and think in ways that are consistent with their rational beliefs and inconsistent with their irrational beliefs.

Ellis (2003) has argued that for the above reasons, a distinct feature of REBT is its emphasis on a philosophy of commitment and effort. In particular, REBT encourages people to commit themselves to make themselves uncomfortable doing things that they don't want to do so that they become comfortable later.

Force and energy in change

As I have stressed here, change involves hard work and clients need to adopt a philosophy of commitment and effort to get the most out of REBT. In so doing they need to use techniques that involve force and energy. Thus, strong disputing of irrational beliefs is said to be more effective than weak disputing and powerfully repeating rational beliefs is deemed to be more effective than repeating them in a weak fashion.

Also, using emotive techniques (i.e. those that actively engage clients' emotions) is preferred to techniques that are less or non-emotive. And using force and energy in behavioural change is deemed to be more helpful than being unforceful and unenergetic. The employment of shame-attacking exercises is a particularly distinctive feature of REBT. Here, clients are encouraged to act "shamefully" in public while accepting themselves unconditionally for so doing. This technique is a good example of an emotive method used with force and energy behaviourally.

When they can, REBT therapists urge clients to integrate emotive and forceful methods with different modalities. As Ellis (2003, p. 233) has said, REBT:

Tries to use its cognitive methods *with* strong emotional and behavioral overtones; it uses its emotional-evocative techniques *with* powerful thinking and behavior; and it uses its behavioral techniques *with* forceful thinking and emotions.

26

Emphasis on teaching clients general rational philosophies and encouraging them to make a profound philosophic change

REBT is distinct among the cognitive-behaviour therapies in encouraging clients to work towards what we call a profound philosophic change. This means, as Ellis (2003, p. 233) has said, that REBT:

> . . . tries to help them acquire several core attitudes that they can use to undisturb themselves in a large number of situations and not merely with the emotional-behavioral problem with which they come to psychotherapy.

The following comprises what we call a profound philosophic change in REBT:

- Having and acting on strong desires, but refraining from transforming these desires into demands on self, others and life, no matter how strong the desires are.
- Acknowledging that it is bad when desires are not met, but not awful.
- Tolerating frustration and discomfort when it is in one's interests to do so.
- Unconditionally accepting oneself warts and all and then resolving to change aspects of self that are negative and that can be changed. This has recently been termed USA (unconditional self-acceptance) by Ellis (e.g. 2003).
- Unconditionally accepting others warts and all and then working to influence these others for the better. This has

recently been termed UOA (unconditional other-acceptance) by Ellis (e.g. 2003) – see Point 11.

• Unconditionally accepting life as a complex mixture of the good, the bad and the neutral and then working to change the bad and capitalise on the good. This has recently been called ULA (unconditional life-acceptance) by Ellis (e.g. 2003) – see Point 11.

Very few people can make this profound philosophic change in all areas of their life (called "superelegant" by Ellis in Weinrach, 1980), let alone maintain it for any length of time. A few clients may achieve such a profound change in most areas of their life and as these areas reduce the greater number of clients achieve it. Most clients tend to achieve a philosophic change in one or two areas of their life and others may make other changes that do not involve belief change (see Point 27).

Both Beck (Padesky & Beck, 2003) and Ellis (2003) agree that REBT and cognitive therapy differ in that the former places much more emphasis on actively teaching general philosophies to clients. Apart from teaching clients the content of such general rational philosophies, REBT therapists teach their client how to change their general irrational philosophies to these general philosophies, sometimes using quite structured exercises in the process (e.g. Dryden, 2001).

Apart from teaching their clients the content of general rational philosophies and how to acquire them cognitively, REBT therapists also teach them how best to integrate these philosophies into their overall belief system. REBT has many emotive and behavioural techniques that its therapists can call upon and some REBT therapists have produced written step-by-step guidance for their use (e.g. Dryden, 2001). Rather than dwell on these techniques here, I want to concentrate on one important point that REBT therapists teach their clients, which provides them with an organising principle for how to get the most out of REBT's cognitive, emotive and behavioural techniques. This principle states that clients will get the most out of

REBT and thereby increase their chances of making a profound philosophic change under the following conditions:

1   When they hold a rational belief and act and think in ways that are consistent with this belief and inconsistent with the irrational alternative to this belief. Here all psychological systems are operating together and in the service of the clients' goals.
2   When they do this in situations that are increasingly aversive either using the flooding principle or the "challenging, but not overwhelming" principle that I discussed in Point 24.
3   When they repeat the above while feeling uncomfortable until they are comfortable with their new rational belief.
4   When they generalise their learning to other relevant situations.
5   When they apply the above four points in all areas of their life.

If so few clients achieve profound philosophic change, why try to help them achieve it?

When I give workshops on REBT and talk about the concept of "profound philosophic change", I am asked the following question, when I mention that so few clients achieve a profound philosophic change: "If so few clients achieve profound philosophic change, why try to help them achieve it?"

My answer is along the following lines:

It is not possible to tell in advance how much change a client is capable of making. If I pre-judge that a client is not capable of making a profound philosophic change and therefore do not try to help them achieve it, then I am depriving them of the possibility of making such a change. Thus, I proceed on the basis that a person is capable of making a profound philosophic change until I gain evidence to the contrary. When I get that evidence, I still try to help them to make the best philosophic change they are in fact capable of making.

It is my view that this approach makes REBT distinctive on this issue among the cognitive-behavioural therapies.

27

Compromises in therapeutic change

As discussed above, REBT encourages clients to make a "profound philosophic change" preferably across the board, but if this is not feasible, then in as many areas as possible and certainly on the problems for which they have been seeking help. The essence of such change is belief change. But what do REBT therapists do when our clients are not able or do not wish to change their beliefs from irrational (rigid and extreme) to rational (flexible and non-extreme)?

The answer lies in REBT's basic adherence to the principle of flexibility. To be more specific, REBT therapists are prepared to make compromises with their preferred therapeutic goals (Dryden, 1987). So, if clients are not going to make belief-based changes, the following changes are available for therapists and clients to consider.

Inference-based change

When we focus our therapeutic efforts on our clients' distorted inferences rather than on their irrational beliefs, we are helping them to stand back and consider the accuracy of these inferences. This very much goes against REBT's usual strategy discussed in Point 20, namely that we first encourage our clients to assume temporarily that their inferences at "A" are true so that we can identify, challenge and change the irrational beliefs that normally underlie these distorted inferences.

For example, Harriet was hurt about her best friend, Susan, not inviting her to her birthday party. Her inference at "A" was: "Susan thinks I'm boring". The usual REBT strategy would be to encourage Harriet to assume temporarily that

Susan did find her boring and then to discover and examine her irrational beliefs about this assumed "fact". However, what if Harriet does not want to do this, is not prepared to do this, is unable to do this or is too disturbed to do this. If we work with her at the inferential level, we do the following:

- Focus on her inference.
- Assist her in collecting information that supports this inference and information that contradicts it and encourage her to write the gathered evidence under separate headings.
- Help her to evaluate this evidence.
- Encourage her to stand back and choose the most probable inference based on the available evidence.
- Suggest that she test out this new inference, if relevant.

Harriet was helped to do this and came to the conclusion that Susan did invite her, but the invitation probably got lost in the post. When she tested this out she did discover that this was exactly what happened.

Once clients have been helped to make an inference-based change they are sometimes more amenable to going back and considering the possibility of making a belief-based change.

Behaviour-based change

Behaviour-based change occurs when clients do not change their irrational beliefs, but improve by effecting constructive changes in their behaviour. Such constructive change occurs under two major conditions:

1   *When clients replace dysfunctional behaviour with construc-tive behaviour.* An example of this is when Fiona learned how to give effective presentations when hitherto her skills at giving them were poor.
2   *When clients acquire constructive patterns of behaviour that have previously been absent from their skill repertoire.* An

example of this is when Peter learned dating skills to help him with women.

In both types of situations, the constructive, behavioural changes that people make help them in two ways. First they help to bring about more positive responses from others. For example, Fiona got better feedback from work colleagues and Peter got more dates from women. Second, they help people develop task confidence, which, in turn, can lead them to make further behavioural changes in related areas.

The downside of these behaviour-based changes without concomitant belief change is that the people concerned are still vulnerable when they face adversities. Thus, Fiona may do well as long as her presentations are well received, but can she cope with poor feedback? And Peter may do well as long as his newly acquired dating skills are also well received, but do they help him to cope with rejection from women who aren't as impressed. The answer to these questions is probably no.

Changing the environment

Perhaps the most obvious example of this type of change is where clients remove themselves physically from the negative situational "A" in which they disturbed themselves. For example, a client who has made himself unhealthily angry about one of his co-workers' racist attitudes, changes his job.

Another common approach to changing the environment is by directly modifying it with the result that clients stop experiencing an unhealthy negative emotion. This involves clients confronting the environment in order to change it rather than avoiding it. An example of this approach is a client who makes herself unhealthily angry about her adolescent children playing music loudly on their hi-fi and who gets rid of her unhealthy angry feelings by taking away the hi-fi system from her children so that they cannot play music loudly.

As with other non-belief-based changes, making environ-mental changes does not help clients to also make belief-based changes since it effectively involves what we call in REBT changing the "A". In general, changing the "A" discourages clients from changing the "B". However, getting away from an aversive environment may provide clients with an opportunity to think more clearly about how they disturbed themselves when they were in the environment and how they could have handled the situation better if they had changed their irrational belief to the alternative rational belief. This may inspire them to return to the aversive environment and practise thinking rationally in the situation. This is a good example of how changing the environment may promote later belief-based change.

28

Focus on clients' misconceptions, doubts, reservations, and objections to REBT

All CBT approaches place due emphasis on helping clients to identify and deal with a variety of obstacles to change (e.g. Dryden & Neenan, 2004a; Leahy, 2001). This has sometimes been referred to as "resistance". What distinguishes REBT in this area is the emphasis it places on helping clients to identify and address their doubts, reservations and objections to the theory, concepts and practices of REBT itself (e.g. Dryden, 2001).

In particular, a number of writers (Dryden, 2004; Gandy, 1985; Saltzberg & Elkins, 1980) have identified a number of misconceptions that clients and therapists (even other CBT therapists!) have about REBT. For example, in his client guide, Dryden (2004) outlined the following client misconceptions:

1 REBT states that events don't cause emotional problems. This is true when negative events are mild or moderate, but not when they are very negative in nature, like being raped or losing a loved one.
2 The principle of emotional responsibility leads to blaming the victim.
3 If I say I disturb myself about your bad behaviour, for example, that will lead you to say that my response has got nothing to do with your behaviour. That is a copout and the principle of emotional responsibility promotes it.
4 The ABC model is overly simplistic.
5 REBT neglects the past.
6 The REBT concept of acceptance encourages complacency.
7 REBT neglects emotions.

8 With its emphasis on techniques, REBT neglects the therapeutic relationship.

9 The therapeutic relationship in REBT is an unequal one.

10 REBT therapists brainwash their clients.

11 REBT therapists tell their clients what to feel and what to do.

12 REBT therapists prevent clients from finding their own solutions to their problems.

13 REBT "straitjackets" clients.

14 REBT is only concerned with changing beliefs.

15 REBT relies heavily on verbal interchange between therapist and client. It also advocates concepts that are difficult to grasp. This means that REBT only works with highly verbal, intelligent clients.

Dryden (2004) encourages REBT therapists to be mindful of the possible existence of such misconceptions that clients may have about REBT and urges them to make these explicit in the therapeutic process, before outlining ways of responding to them.

Responding to misconceptions: An example

Here is an example of how to respond to one such misconception:

Misconception

REBT states that events don't cause emotions. I can see that this is the case when negative events are mild or moderate, but don't very negative events like being raped or losing a loved one cause disturbed emotions?

Possible therapist response

Your question directly impinges on the distinction that REBT makes between healthy and unhealthy negative emotions Let me take the example of rape that you mentioned. There is no doubt that being raped is a tragic event for both women and men. As such, it is healthy for the person who has been raped to experience a lot of distress. However, REBT conceptualises this distress as healthy even though it is intense. Other approaches to therapy have as their goal the reduction of the intensity of negative emotions. They take this position because they do not keenly differentiate between healthy negative emotions (distress) and unhealthy negative emotions (disturbance).

Now, REBT keenly distinguishes between healthy distress and unhealthy disturbance. Healthy distress stems from your rational beliefs about a negative activating event, while disturbance stems from your irrational beliefs about the same event. I now have to introduce you to one of the complexities of REBT theory and as I do you will see that REBT is not always as simple as ABC!

REBT theory holds that the intensity of your healthy distress increases in proportion to the negativity of the event that you face and the strength of your rational beliefs. Now, when a person has been raped, her (in this case) intense distress stems from her strongly held rational beliefs about this very negative A. As virtually everyone who has been raped will have strongly held rational beliefs about this event, we could almost say that being raped "causes" intense healthy distress.

Now let me introduce irrational beliefs into the picture. REBT theory argues that you, being human, easily transmute your rational beliefs into irrational beliefs especially when the events you encounter are very negative. However, and this is a crucial and controversial point, the specific principle of emotional responsibility states that you are largely responsible for your emotional disturbance because you are responsible for transmuting your rational beliefs into irrational beliefs. You (and others) retain this responsibility even when you (they) encounter tragic adversities such as rape. So, REBT theory holds that when a person has been raped, she is responsible for transmuting her strongly held rational beliefs into irrational beliefs, even though it is very understandable that she should do this.

Actually, if we look at the typical irrational beliefs that people have about being raped, we will see that these beliefs are not an integral part of the rape experience, but reflect what people bring to the experience. Examples of irrational beliefs are:

- "I absolutely should have stopped this from happening."
- "This has completely ruined my life."
- "Being raped means that I am a worthless person."

While it is understandable that people who have been raped should think this way, this does not detract from the fact that they are responsible for bringing these irrational beliefs to the experience. It is for this reason that REBT theory holds that very negative "A"s do not "cause" emotional disturbance. This is actually an optimistic position. If very negative events did cause emotional disturbance then you would have a much harder time overcoming your disturbed feelings than you do now when we make the assumption that these feelings stem largely from your irrational beliefs. One more point. Some REBT therapists distinguish between disturbed emotions that are experienced when a very negative event occurs and disturbed feelings that persist well after the event has happened. These therapists would argue that being raped does "cause" disturbed feelings when the event occurs and for a short period after it has happened, but if the person's disturbed feelings persist well after the event then the person who has been raped is responsible for the perpetuation of her disturbances via the creation and perpetuation of her irrational beliefs. These therapists argue that time-limited irrationalities in response to very negative activating events are not unhealthy reactions, but the perpetuation of these irrationalities is unhealthy. Thus, for these REBT therapists a very negative event like rape does "cause" emotional disturbance in the short term, but not in the long term.

Please note that while I have presented this response as if the therapist is lecturing the client, in practice he or she would fully engage the client in a discussion of the relevant issues. The above presentation is constrained by the book's format, which limits the publication of very lengthy therapist–client dialogue.

I have provided suggestions for how to respond to all the misconceptions listed above elsewhere (see Dryden, 2004).

Doubts, reservations and objections to particular aspects of REBT theory and practice

Apart from these misconceptions, REBT therapists are also on the look out for the possible presence of a number of clients' doubts, reservations and objections to particular aspects of REBT theory and practice. When they are found they are explicitly discussed and dealt with, thus freeing clients to get the most out of REBT. Here are some common doubts, reservations and objections:

1   Doubts, reservations and objections to adopting rational beliefs (i.e. flexible beliefs, anti-awfulising beliefs, HFT beliefs and/or acceptance beliefs) and to giving up irrational beliefs (i.e. rigid beliefs, awfulising beliefs, LFT beliefs and/ or depreciation beliefs).
2   Doubts, reservations and objections to adopting healthy negative emotions and to giving up unhealthy negative emotions.
3   Doubts, reservations and objections to adopting constructive behaviour and to giving up unconstructive behaviour.

See Dryden (2001) for examples of how to deal with such doubts, reservations and objections.

29

Therapeutic efficiency

Albert Ellis has always been interested in efficiency both in life and in psychotherapy. A distinctive feature of REBT, therefore, is the emphasis that it places on efficiency in its practice. In a seminal paper, Ellis (1980c) specified several criteria of psychotherapeutic efficiency. None of these criteria on its own defines REBT's distinctive contribution. This is defined by all seven in concert.

Brevity

REBT therapists aim to help clients in the shortest time possible. This is why we endeavour to teach clients to use the skills of REBT to help themselves. We do this to save therapists time and clients money. However, we also realise that some clients who are really quite disturbed cannot be helped briefly.

Depth-centredness

One of REBT's distinctive features is its early focus on irrational beliefs (see Point 20). It argues that irrational (i.e. rigid and extreme) beliefs are at the core of psychological disturbance and therefore clients can be helped as quickly as possible to identify, challenge and change these beliefs and develop and practise rational alternatives to these beliefs.

Pervasiveness

Pervasiveness in psychotherapy is defined as "the therapists helping the clients to deal with many of their problems, and in a sense their whole lives, rather than with a few presenting symptoms" (Ellis, 1980c, p. 415). While other CBT therapies recognise that a client's problems are underpinned by a number of core beliefs (known as core irrational beliefs in REBT), REBT not only endeavours to help clients to zero in and change their core irrational beliefs as soon as is feasible it endeavours to teach clients a rational self-helping philosophy that they can apply across the board.

Extensiveness

As Ellis (1980c) has noted, extensiveness means helping clients not only to minimise their disturbed feelings, but also to promote their potential for happy living. REBT is best placed to do this among the CBT therapies as it has been used extensively both in clinical and personal development settings.

Thoroughgoingness

REBT uses a plethora of cognitive, emotive and behavioural techniques in a thoroughgoing manner. It may not be as comprehensive as multimodal therapy (Lazarus, 1981), but it runs it close.

Maintaining therapeutic progress

REBT argues that once clients have made progress in therapy they have to work hard to maintain this progress. In particular, REBT is fairly unique among the CBT therapies in highlighting the philosophy of low frustration tolerance (LFT) in being a prime obstacle to therapeutic progress. REBT focuses clients on this philosophy and encourages them to develop a philosophy of high frustration tolerance to help them to maintain and even enhance their therapeutic progress.

Promotion of prevention

An efficient psychotherapy not only helps clients to deal with the emotional problems that they have, it also helps them to prevent the development of future problems. REBT does this by:

- Teaching clients to identify their vulnerabilities and the themes that define them (e.g. failure, being rejected, etc.).
- Helping them to identify, challenge and change the irrational beliefs that underpin these vulnerabilities.
- Encouraging them to develop constructive behaviours and realistic modes of thinking that they can implement as a way of reinforcing their developing rational beliefs.
- Suggesting that they practise healthy ways of thinking and acting before they enter and while they are facing situations in which they are liable to disturb themselves.
- Urging them to seek out increasingly difficult situations to confront in which they would normally disturb themselves, but instead rehearse healthy beliefs and act and think in ways that are constructive and realistic.

30

Theoretically consistent eclecticism

REBT is a form of what I have called theoretically consistent eclecticism (Dryden, 1986). This means that REBT therapists are encouraged to draw broadly from a variety of therapeutic approaches but in ways that are consistent with REBT theory. Don't forget that in this book I am particularly discussing the specific form of REBT – rather than its general form which is, as Ellis (1980a) has argued, indistinguishable from CBT. When practising general REBT, REBT therapists will draw liberally from other approaches, particularly other CBT approaches and when we do so, we are less concerned about the consistency of what we borrow with REBT theory.

In all probability, different REBT therapists take different things from different approaches and as such there are different "flavours" of theoretically consistent eclectic therapy. To demonstrate this, let me briefly outline what I routinely borrow from other approaches.

Windy Dryden's brand of eclectic REBT

In this section I will briefly discuss the following: working alliance therapy, cognitive therapy, experiential approaches and mindfulness meditation.

Working alliance theory

Bordin (1979) has been credited with being the pioneer of this framework. He argued that the alliance between clients and therapists has a number of components:

- *bonds* (the interpersonal connectedness between clients and therapists);
- *goals* (what clients want to achieve from therapy and what their therapists want them to achieve); and
- *tasks* (what clients and therapists do to help clients to achieve their goals).

Bordin (1979) has argued that effective therapy is more likely to occur when the bonds between clients and therapists are strong and enable both to work together, when clients and therapists agree with the goals of therapy and when both are willing and able to carry out the tasks that are potent enough to help clients to achieve their goals.

I use this framework to guide my general strategies and specific strategies. I have also suggested a fourth component, which I call "views", that focuses on the ideas both clients and therapists have about what determines the clients' problems, how these can best be ameliorated and other salient aspects of the therapeutic endeavour (Dryden, 2006). Here, effective therapy is more likely to occur when clients and therapists have similar views about therapy.

Cognitive therapy

I particularly find the concepts of agenda setting and developing a problem list that originated in cognitive therapy (Beck et al., 1979) helpful, especially with clients who are cognitively and emotionally disorganised and those who jump from problem to problem and topic to topic. Such procedures provide greater structure to REBT and it is interesting to see that both Beck (Padesky & Beck, 2003) and Ellis (2003) agree that the routine practice of cognitive therapy is more structured than the routine practice of REBT.

Experiential approaches

I employ techniques from experiential approaches to therapy like gestalt therapy mainly to help clients to identify feelings and thoughts that are difficult to identify employing usual assessment methods. Focusing methods (Gendlin, 1978) are particularly useful in identifying feelings and two-chair methods from gestalt therapy (Passons, 1975) are useful in helping to identify thoughts because they are required to articulate them during the technique.

I should add that, consistent with REBT theory, I do not think that such methods are therapeutic in themselves, but in the assistance that they provide in helping me practise specific REBT when usual methods fail.

Mindfulness meditation

The use of mindfulness meditation (Kabat-Zinn, 1990) is increasing in CBT, initially in the treatment of recurrent depression (Segal, Williams, & Teasdale, 2002) and latterly in other disorders. The purpose of this approach to meditation is to help clients not to engage with harmful thoughts but to let them pass through their mind. I use such methods *after* I have encouraged clients to dispute their irrational beliefs and when they are still holding distorted inferences at "C" in the ABC framework that persist even when these inferences have been questioned.

Techniques that are avoided in REBT

So far I have discussed the use of techniques within the theoretically consistent eclectic practice of REBT. It is also useful to consider what techniques are not employed in REBT even within its eclectic practice (Dryden & Neenan, 2004b).

129

1   Techniques that help people become more dependent, e.g. undue therapist warmth as a strong reinforcement and the creation and analysis of a transference neurosis.
2   Techniques that encourage people to become more gullible and suggestible, e.g. Pollyannaish positive thinking.
3   Techniques that are long winded and inefficient, e.g. psychoanalytic methods in general and free association in particular; encouraging clients to give lengthy descriptions of activating experiences at "A".
4   Methods that help people feel better in the short term rather than get better in the long term (Ellis, 1972), e.g. some experiental techniques like fully expressing one's feelings in a dramatic, cathartic and abreactive manner, i.e. some gestalt methods and primal techniques. The danger here is that such methods may encourage people to practise irrational philosophies underlying such emotions as anger.
5   Techniques that distract clients from working on their irrational philosophies, e.g. relaxation methods, yoga and other cognitive distraction methods. These methods may be employed, however, *along with* cognitive disputing designed to yield some philosophic change.
6   Methods that may unwittingly reinforce clients' philosophy of low frustration tolerance, e.g. gradual desensitisation (see Point 24).
7   Techniques that include an anti-scientific philosophy, e.g. faith healing and mysticism.
8   Techniques that attempt to change activating events ("A") before or without showing clients how to change their irrational beliefs ("B"), e.g. some strategic family systems techniques.
9   Techniques that have dubious validity, e.g. neurolinguistic programming.

Having said this, it is important to note that REBT therapists do not avoid using the above methods in any absolute sense.

We may, on certain restricted occasions with certain clients, utilise such techniques, particularly for pragmatic purposes. For example, if faith healing is the only method that will prevent some clients from harming themselves, then we might either employ it ourselves or, more probably, refer such clients to a faith healer (Ellis, 2002). This shows the relativistic core of REBT, which is perhaps its most distinctive feature!

References

Barzun, J. (1964) *Of Human Freedom*. Philadelphia: Lippincott.

Beck, A. T. (1976) *Cognitive Therapy and the Emotional Disorders*. New York: International Universities Press.

Beck, A. T. (2002, June 4) *The Word "Challenge"*. Academy of Cognitive Therapy Listserve Posting.

Beck, A. T., Rush, A. J., Shaw, B. F. and Emery, G. (1979) *Cognitive Therapy of Depression*. New York: Guilford Press.

Bordin, E. S. (1979) 'The generalizability of the psychoanalytic concept of the working alliance', *Psychotherapy: Theory, Research and Practice*, 16: 252–260.

DiGiuseppe, R. (1991a) 'A rational-emotive model of assessment', in M. Bernard (ed.), *Using Rational-Emotive Therapy Effectively*. New York: Plenum Press.

DiGiuseppe, R. (1991b) 'Comprehensive cognitive disputing in rational-emotive therapy', in M. Bernard (ed.), *Using Rational-Emotive Therapy Effectively*. New York: Plenum Press.

Dobson, K. S. (ed.) (2001) *Handbook of Cognitive-Behavioral Therapies*, 2nd edn. New York: Guilford Press.

Dryden, W. (1985) 'Challenging but not overwhelming: A compromise in negotiating homework assignments', *British Journal of Cognitive Psychotherapy*, 3(1): 77–80.

Dryden, W. (1986) 'A case of theoretically consistent eclecticism: Humanizing a computer "addict"', *International Journal of Eclectic Psychotherapy*, 5(4), 309–327.

Dryden, W. (1987) 'Compromises in rational-emotive therapy', in W. Dryden, *Current Issues in Rational-Emotive Therapy*. London: Croom Helm.

Dryden, W. (1997) *Therapists' Dilemmas*, revised edn. London: Sage.

Dryden, W. (1998) 'Understanding persons in the context of their problems: A rational emotive behaviour therapy perspective', in M. Bruch and F. W. Bond (eds), *Beyond Diagnosis: Case Formulation Approaches in CBT*. Chichester, UK: Wiley.

Dryden, W. (1999) 'Beyond LFT and discomfort disturbance: The case for the term "non-ego disturbance"', *Journal of Rational-Emotive and Cognitive-Behavior Therapy*, 17(3): 165–200.

Dryden, W. (2001) *Reason to Change: A Rational Emotive Behaviour Therapy (REBT) Workbook*. Hove, UK: Brunner-Routledge.

Dryden, W. (2002) *Fundamentals of Rational Emotive Behaviour Therapy: A Training Handbook*. London: Whurr.

Dryden, W. (2004) *Rational Emotive Behaviour Therapy: Clients' Manual*. London: Whurr.

Dryden, W. (2006) *Counselling in a Nutshell*. London: Sage.

Dryden, W., Gordon, J. and Neenan, M. (1997) *What is Rational Emotive Behaviour Therapy? A Personal and Practical Guide*. Loughton, UK: Gale Centre Publications.

Dryden, W. and Neenan, M. (2004a) *The Rational Emotive Behavioural Approach to Therapeutic Change*. London: Sage.

Dryden, W. and Neenan, M. (2004b) *Counselling Individuals: A Rational Emotive Behavioural Handbook*. London: Whurr.

Ellis, A. (1962) *Reason and Emotion in Psychotherapy*. Secaucus, NJ: Lyle Stuart.

Ellis, A. (1972) 'Helping people get better: Rather than merely feel better', *Rational Living*, 7(2): 2–9.

Ellis, A. (1976) 'The biological basis of human irrationality', *Journal of Individual Psychology*, 32: 145–168.

Ellis, A. (1978) 'Toward a theory of personality', in R. J. Corsini (ed.), *Readings in Current Personality Theories*. Itasca, IL: Peacock.

Ellis, A. (1979) 'Discomfort anxiety: A new cognitive behavioural construct. Part I', *Rational Living*, 14(2): 3–8.

Ellis, A. (1980a) 'Rational-emotive therapy and cognitive behavior therapy: Similarities and differences', *Cognitive Therapy and Research*, 4: 325–340.

Ellis, A. (1980b) 'Discomfort anxiety: A new cognitive behavioral construct. Part 2', *Rational Living*, 15(1): 25–30.

Ellis, A. (1980c) 'The value of efficiency in psychotherapy', *Psychotherapy: Theory, Research and Practice*, 17: 414–418.

Ellis, A. (1983a) *The case against religiosity*. New York: Albert Ellis Institute.

Ellis, A. (1983b) 'The philosophic implications and dangers of some popular behavior therapy techniques', in M. Rosenbaum, C. M. Franks and Y. Jaffe (eds), *Perspectives in Behavior Therapy in the Eighties*. New York: Springer.

Ellis, A. (1987) 'The use of rational humorous songs in psychotherapy', in W. F. Fry, Jr. and W. A. Salameh (eds), *Handbook of Humor in Psychotherapy: Advances in the Clinical Use of Humor*. Sarasota, FL: Professional Resource Exchange, Inc.

Ellis, A. (1994) *Reason and Emotion in Psychotherapy*, revised and updated edn. New York: Birch Lane Press.

Ellis, A. (2002) *Overcoming Resistance: A Rational Emotive Behavior Therapy Integrated Approach*, 2nd edn. New York: Springer.

Ellis, A. (2003) 'Similarities and differences between rational emotive behavior therapy and cognitive therapy', *Journal of Cognitive Psychotherapy: An International Quarterly*, 17: 225–240.

Ellis, A. (2004) *Rational Emotive Behaviour Therapy: It Works For Me – It Can Work For You*. New York: Prometheus Books.

Ellis, A. and Dryden, W. (1997) *The Practice of Rational Emotive Behavior Therapy*, 2nd edn. New York: Springer.

Freud, A. (1937) *The Ego and the Mechanisms of Defence*. London: Hogarth.

Gandy, G. L. (1985) 'Frequent misperceptions of rational-emotive therapy: An overview for the rehabilitation counselor', *Journal of Applied Rehabilitation Counseling*, 16(4): 31–35.

Gendlin, E. T. (1978) *Focusing*. New York: Everest House.

Grieger, R. M. and Boyd, J. (1980) *Rational-Emotive Therapy: A Skills-based Approach*. New York: Van Nostrand Reinhold.

Hjelle, L. A. and Ziegler, D. J. (1992) *Personality Theories: Basic Assumptions, Research and Applications*. New York: McGraw-Hill.

Kabat-Zinn, J. (1990) *Full Catastrophe Living: Using the Wisdom of Your Mind and Your Body to Face Stress, Pain and Illness*. New York: Dell Publishing.

Korzybski, A. (1933) *Science and Society*. San Francisco: ISGS.

Lazarus, A. A. (1981) *The Practice of Multimodal Therapy*. New York: McGraw-Hill.

Leahy, R. L. (2001) *Overcoming Resistance in Cognitive Therapy*. New York: Guilford Press.

Maslow, A. (1968) *Toward a Psychology of Being*. New York: Van Nostrand Reinhold.

Padesky, C. A. and Beck, A. T. (2003) 'Science and philosophy: Comparison of cognitive therapy and rational emotive behaviour therapy', *Journal of Cognitive Psychotherapy: An International Quarterly*, 17: 211–224.

Passons, W. R. (1975) *Gestalt Approaches in Counseling.* New York: Holt Rinehart & Winston.

Persons, J. (1989) *Cognitive Therapy: A Case Formulation Approach.* New York: Norton.

Reivich, K. and Shatte, A. (2002) *The Resilience Factor: 7 Keys to Finding your Inner Strength and Overcoming Life's Hurdles.* New York: Broadway Books.

Rogers, C. R. (1957) 'The necessary and sufficient conditions of therapeutic personality change', *Journal of Consulting Psychology*, *21*, 95–103.

Saltzberg, L. and Elkins, G. R. (1980) 'An examination of common concerns about rational-emotive therapy', *Professional Psychology: Research and Practice*, 11(2): 324–330.

Segal, Z. V., Williams, J. M. G. and Teasdale, J. D. (2002) *Mindfulness-based Cognitive Therapy for Depression.* New York: Guilford Press.

Walen, S. R., DiGiuseppe, R. and Dryden, W. (1992) *A Practitioner's Guide to Rational-Emotive Therapy*, 2nd edn. New York: Oxford University Press.

Weinrach, S. G. (1980) 'Unconventional therapist: Albert Ellis', *Personnel and Guidance Journal*, 59: 152–160.

Wessler, R. A. and Wessler, R. L. (1980) *The Principles and Practice of Rational-Emotive Therapy.* San Francisco: Jossey-Bass.

Wolpe, J. (1958) *Psychotherapy by Reciprocal Inhibition.* Stanford, CA: Stanford University Press.

Young, J. E. and Klosko, J. S. (1993) *Reinventing Your Life: The Breakthrough Program to End Negative Behavior And Feel Great Again.* New York: Plume.

Ziegler, D. J. (2000) 'Basic assumptions concerning human nature underlying rational emotive behaviour therapy (REBT) personality theory', *Journal of Rational-Emotive and Cognitive-Behavior Therapy*, 18: 67–85.

Index

The abbreviation REBT is used for Rational Emotive Behaviour Therapy.

responsibility acceptance, for emotional disturbances 65

rigidity of belief: and the attempted exclusion of events 18; creation of rigid and extreme ideas from desires 17–18, 58–9, 63; early focus of rigid beliefs 87–8; extreme beliefs derived from 21–3; irrationality and the ease of 58–9; psychological disturbance and 17–18; *see also* irrationality

risk taking, calculated 68

Rogers, C. R. 71

scientific thinking 66

self-acceptance 44–5, 46, 109

self-demands 43, 47–8

self-depreciation (SD) 47

self-direction 8, 67

self-interest, enlightened 66

shame-attacking exercises 106–7

sin and sinners 14

Situational ABC model 15–16

social action 67

Socratic style of therapy 81, 100

Stoicism 9–10

subjectivity: influence of subjective factors 8

systematic desensitisation 103

systemic emphasis of REBT 14

teaching clients in REBT 79–82; discrimination between irrational and rational beliefs 89–91; rational philosophies for profound philosophical change 109–12

theoretical emphases of REBT: addressing misconceptions 117–21; affective-experiential 10; basic assumptions about human nature 7–9; behavioural 10–11 *see also* behaviour; on beliefs *see* beliefs; constructivistic 12; on emotions *see* emotions; existential-humanistic 12; general semantics 12–14; phenomenological 9; psychodynamic 11–12; psychological interactionist 11; religiosity and 14; Situational ABC model 15–16; Stoic 9–10; systemic 14

therapeutic practice: addressing misconceptions about REBT 117–21; assessment *see* assessment; brevity 123; 'challenging, but not overwhelming' principle of 104; commitment and effort in 105–6; depth-centredness 123; discouragement of gradualism 103–4; disputing beliefs 90–2, 93–7; early focus of irrational beliefs 87–8; efficiency in 123–5; extensiveness 124; facilitating change from irrational to rational beliefs 89–92, 93–7; flexibility and compromise in 113–16; force and energy in 106–7; handling doubts, reservations and objections 121; order of dealing with problems 83–5; pervasiveness 123–4; prevention promotion 125; psycho-education 79–82 *see also* education; styles 99–101; techniques avoided in REBT 129–31; theoretically consistent eclecticism in 127–9; thoroughgoingness 124

INDEX

therapeutic relationship 71–3;
    working alliance theory 127–8
therapists: therapist acceptance
    71–2; therapist warmth 71

uncertainty tolerance 67
unconditional acceptance: of
    complexity of life 30–1, 110; of
    others/humans 40–1, 46,
    109–10; of self 44–5, 46, 109;
    in the therapeutic relationship
    71–2
unconditional human worth 41,
    72
Understanding the Person in the
    Context their Problems
    (UPCP) 76–7

unhealthy negative emotions
    (UNEs) 33–4, 53–5
unhealthy positive emotions
    (UPEs) 34–5
UPCP (Understanding the Person
    in the Context their Problems)
    76–7
Utopianism, healthy rejection of
    66

Wolpe, J. 103
working alliance theory
    127–8

Ziegler, D. J. 7, 9(Fig.)

143